Enjoy Wine

David Biggs
Dave Hughes

Enjoy Wine

STRUIK
TIMMINS

Published by Struik Timmins
(a member of The Struik Group (Pty) Ltd)
Struik House
Oswald Pirow Street
Foreshore
Cape Town
8001

Reg. No. 54/00965/07
First published in 1990
© Struik Timmins
Text © David Biggs and David Hughes
Illustrations © David Biggs

Editor Sean Fraser
Cover designer Robert Meas
Designer Robert Meas
Illustrator David Biggs
Cover illustration Gordon Linley
DTP Co-ordinator Suzanne Fortescue
Reproduction BellSet, Cape Town
Cover reproduction Fotoplate (Pty) Ltd, Cape Town
Printing and binding National Book Printers, Goodwood

ISBN 0 86978 503 6

CONTENTS

Cheers!

FOREWORD

There are already dozens of South African books on wine. It's a subject that fascinates so many people. Most of these books fall into two distinct categories - the elegant coffee-table books of colour photographs (the Cape Winelands are beautiful!) and the serious works on wine recognition, history and appreciation.

But, somewhere along the line, people seem to have forgotten that wine is made for pleasure, fun and enjoyment.

Like most South African wine books, South African wine drinkers fall into categories. At the top end of the social scale there are the sniffers and sippers, who regard wine as a necessary part of social and business life, and cringe at the thought of serving wine at the incorrect temperature or in the wrong glass. Good grief, it would be as devastating as arriving at the opera in brown shoes!

And, at the bottom of the social scale, there are those (the majority of our wine customers, alas) who drink wine to get drunk as quickly and as cheaply as possible.

This book will probably be of no interest at all to anyone in either of these categories. It has been written for people who enjoy the simple pleasure of sharing a glass of good wine with friends.

Even for them, however, there are sometimes problems. Faced with over 3 000 wines on the market, what does one choose? Is it necessary to spend more than R10 on a bottle of wine to ensure that it's a good one? Are Estate wines better than Co-op wines? These are some of the questions we hope to answer.

We both believe that wine enjoyment should be a relaxed business, completely free of social pressure and pretention. That's the way we enjoy it ourselves, and we hope this book will help you to enjoy wine as much as we do.

Cheers!

David Biggs and Dave Hughes

Eat, drink and be merry.

INTRODUCTION

WINE IS FOR FUN

More nonsense is written and spoken about wine than about any other subject - with the possible exception of sex.

Wine 'fundis' happily reel off an endless list of ridiculous rules for drinking wine.

Wine, they will tell you in all earnestness and with a perfectly straight face, must be swirled gently in an anti-clockwise direction before sniffing it. Red wine should be allowed to 'breathe' for a few hours before it is tasted. Sparkling wine corks should not be popped, as this shocks the wine. Red wines should never be chilled and all wines should be stored at exactly 15 degrees celsius.

And so on, ad nauseam.

Some of these 'rules' are based on sound reasoning, but the danger of having rules is that many people make a fetish of them, and forget the real reason for drinking wine.

There is only one valid reason for drinking wine, and that is to enjoy it. Wine should be fun, and drinking it should be a pleasure.

If you drink wine to impress your friends, or to show how cultured you are, or for any other reason than simply to enjoy it, you may be missing out on one of life's finest pleasures.

Of course, there are many levels of enjoyment of every one of life's pleasures.

Two people may look at Botticelli's painting of the *Birth of Venus* and appreciate it on completely different levels. One may whistle and say: 'Jislaaik, that doll's got a big bum. Nice tits, though'. And the other might be absorbed by the creative use of colour and light, or the subtle composition and mood. Who gets the most enjoyment from the painting?

Similarly, two people may taste the same wine and one might find it simply 'lekker' without thinking about why, while the other discovers that it has a very subtle balance between the acid and the fruitiness, or finds that the hint of woodiness is just enough to add interest to an otherwise ordinary wine. The appreciation of fine wine lies not in a wagging tongue, but in the palate.

In this book, we hope to remove some of the sillier myths and pretentions and introduce newcomers to the simple delights of wine.

AS YOU LIKE IT

Despite what the snobs may tell you, there is nothing sacred about wine. It is an agricultural product which is processed and sold to customers, just like jam or biltong.

And once you've bought it, you may do with it what you like. In Italy they mix red wine with orange juice and call it *sangria*, and delicious it is too. Mozambicans like a little Coca-Cola with their wine, to give it bubbles. The Swiss warm their wine and add spices to make *gluhwein*.

Unlike jam or biltong, wine comes in an almost endless variety of flavours and styles. If you compare a syrupy sweet Jerepigo to a well-aged bottle of Cabernet Sauvignon or a yeasty dry Champagne, you'd never guess they are all the product of the same fruit.

This amazing variety is probably the main reason for an almost universal fascination with wine. Given such a vast range from which to choose, there simply MUST be something for every palate. In South Africa alone there are more than 3 000 locally produced wines on the market - and all of them change subtly from vintage to vintage.

In this book, we hope to help you enjoy them all just a little more.

IN THE BEGINNING

EXPLORING THE ORIGINS OF WINE

Nobody knows for certain just when wine was made for the first time. There is archaeological evidence that wine was made in Asia Minor more than 12 000 years ago.

Egyptian tomb paintings show detailed records of winemaking, and their cellar records show that some vintages of wine were considered superior to others.

Many countries have their own legendary tales of the discovery of wine, but the story of Gilga, the shy harem lady, is probably the most popular.

GILGA

Many centuries ago there lived a Middle Eastern king called Amurabi, who was exceptionally fond of fruit.

Unfortunately, in that part of the world, the summer is very hot, so fruit does not last long once it is picked. So Amurabi summoned his wise men and ordered them to seek a way of preserving fruit so that it could be enjoyed all year. As a reward, he promised that anybody who found a suitable preservation method would be given the pick of the royal harem women.

Amurabi, like all kings worthy of the title, had a substantial harem and used to stroll among the lovely ladies every evening, chatting and joking and being fed tasty morsels, until he selected a companion for the night. This was a coveted privilege, as the companion was often given a pretty gift of jewellery or perfume if she pleased Amurabi well.

But one of his newest wives, a shy young maiden called Gilga, was always overlooked because she couldn't bring herself to compete with the other harem women, who would dance and flutter their eyelashes at him seductively, in order to attract his attention.

Gilga loved Amurabi dearly, however, and longed to share his

The fair Gilga~a "shy" maiden?

bed. Eventually she began to despair of ever being noticed by her lord, and began to pine.

Meanwhile, one of the king's wise men concluded that it was the sunlight that caused fruit to spoil. He reasoned that the way to preserve fruit was to keep it in a dark place, where the sunlight could not reach it. So he packed two enormous clay jars full of grapes, sealed them with wax and stored them in the cellar.

Eventually he announced that he was ready to have his theory tested, and King Amurabi commanded that the grapes be brought to him. But when the royal taster took a mouthful of the evilly bubbling mixture in the jars, he gagged and spat and declared the mixture to be poison. He urged Amurabi to throw the poison away and punish the wise man who had made it.

But every Middle Eastern king has his enemies, and one never knows when a jar of potent poison may be handy, so Amurabi labelled the jars clearly to prevent accidents, and had them stored in the deepest dungeon for possible later use.

Back in the harem, young Gilga had become so depressed by her failure to attract Amurabi's attention, that she decided to end her miserable life.

She crept into the deepest dungeon, drew a sharp dagger from her belt and was about to plunge it into her shapely breast, when she noticed the jars marked 'POISON'. Rather than ruin a good robe, she decided to poison herself instead. She drank a cup of the poison and sat down, weeping, and waited to die.

Nothing happened. So she took a second cup and again waited to die, now feeling rather better, and no longer weeping.

After the third cup, she decided that dying might not be such a good idea after all. In fact, she decided to tell Amurabi just what she thought of his continued rejection.

Young Gilga marched into the royal bedchamber, grasped the king's companion for the night by the hair and tossed her from the room. She then proceeded to tell the king several facts about himself and herself, and ended by showing him some very uninhibited tricks that both astonished and delighted him.

The next morning, when Amurabi asked Gilga what had caused her transformation, she told him the secret of the 'poison' in the cellar. From that moment she became his favourite, and he ordered that the wonderful grape poison be served whenever he and Gilga were alone together.

Who knows, the story may even be true.

What probably is true is that wine was discovered, rather than invented. You may hear of people making wine from almost any fruit or vegetable from parsnips to dandelions. But when we talk of 'wine' we mean the fermented juice of the grape. Grapes contain all the ingredients needed to make wine, and grapes have been used for many centuries for this purpose.

The Greeks and Romans have a proud history of wine consumption, but although they were passionate wine drinkers, their uninhibited drinking habits would be considered a little unusual, even by today's standards.

Like the Romans, the Greeks preferred a strong and heavy wine. Naturally, these concentrated beverages were often diluted with either pure drinking water or even sea water. The salt would then conceal any fault which may have occurred in the winemaking process. Of course, today's connoisseur would rather go thirsty than allow his wine and his palate to be insulted so.

BACCHUS

Literature is crammed with tales of wine, its origin and the path of destruction down which it has led mankind. The history of wine and the role it has played in the development of culture is an interesting one. Many of our fables, myths and legends are intricately woven around wine and man's passion for the fruit of the vine.

According to Greco-Roman mythology, the god of wine, fertility and merriment was the great Bacchus. Also known as Dionysus, Bacchus represented the life-blood of life, 'the keeper of the vine' and, quite naturally, 'the giver of ecstasy'. Although Bacchus spent much of his life carrying vines and the time-honoured secrets of winemaking to foreign lands, he was constantly accompanied by a party of wild and lusty centaurs, satyrs and loose women.

As can be expected, this ancient god of festivity and debauchery had no shortage of followers, and was particularly popular among the peasant classes of Roman society. In fact, the Bacchanalia, the most popular of the Roman holidays, became little more than an excuse for wild parties and depravity - and was eventually banned by the Senate. There was nothing sacred or holy about Bacchus, God of Wine, and his history is scattered with bawdy symbols of excess and immorality. But such is the history of mankind, is it not?

THE SOUTH AFRICAN WINE STORY

THE HISTORY AND THE HERITAGE

It is not necessary to know the entire history of the South African wine industry to appreciate or enjoy wine, but it may be interesting to have a few facts on hand.

If you want to study the subject in more detail, there are plenty of excellent publications available.

The first wine was made at the Cape in 1659, only seven years after Jan van Riebeeck had landed here to start a new settlement. The colony was established to supply sailors and merchants with fresh food and water. Little did the Dutch realise that their 'refreshment station' would soon be producing some of the finest wines the world has seen.

However, a fact often ignored by wine lovers is that beer was brewed at the Cape before wine was made. Wine enthusiasts are quick to quote van Riebeeck's famous diary entry: "Today, God be praised, wine was pressed at the Cape for the first time."

He recorded the first beer being brewed earlier, but didn't think it worth praising God for that.

So there.

The wine industry was given a valuable boost by the arrival of the French Huguenot settlers, who brought with them, not only their refined culture, but also their fine skill in winemaking.

The French Huguenots established magnificent farms in the Franschhoek valley and the French tradition lives on today in the names of the historical farms - La Motte, La Provence, L'Ormarins, and Clos Cabrière.

Groot Constantia, established by Governor Simon van der Stel, became known throughout the civilised world for its fine, sweet wines. It is reported that the ailing Napoleon called for a bottle of Constantia wine on his death-bed. Unfortunately, there are no accurate records of that early winemaking, so we can only guess at the style of those famous wines.

First there was the grape.
and the rest is history.

The British, who occupied the Cape in 1795, gave preferential treatment to Cape wines, as they were on the warpath with the French at the time. As a result, the Cape wine industry flourished.

SOUR GRAPES

Then, in 1885, the whole industry collapsed with the discovery of an aphid called phylloxera in the Cape vineyards.

Tragedy struck. The disaster was total, and the determined creature wiped out the entire industry. Fortunately for wine lovers, however, it was discovered that wild American grape varieties were immune to attack from phylloxera, and a new start was made, using European vines grafted to American root stocks.

This practice is still followed in the Cape winelands today.

By 1918 the Cape wine industry was again in trouble, this time mainly due to serious over-production and a lack of quality control.

The KWV (the Co-operative Winegrowers' Association) was established to act as a controlling body, a role it continues to play.

One of the main functions of the KWV is to exercise some form of control over the production of wine, and it does this by granting wine production quotas to producers. Farmers may only produce grapes for winemaking if they are in possession of the necessary permit issued by the KWV.

The organisation also determines the minimum prices to be paid for wines each year. The 'floor price' was introduced to guarantee wine farmers a reasonable income. To protect the market from surplus production, the KWV buys grapes from producers and makes natural wines for export only.

It also buys distilling wine for the production of brandy and fortified wines, and only some are available on the local market.

The KWV plays an important role in promoting the sale of South African wines in other countries, and runs regular wine courses at its farm, Laborie, in Paarl.

TODAY'S SCENE

Today there are various types of wine producers in the country. Most of the popular wines are made by large merchant wholesalers, such as the Stellenbosch Farmers' Winery and Distillers' Corporation, who supply many of the country's best-known branded wines -

Zonnebloem, Fleur du Cap, Tassenberg, Nederburg and Virginia.

These large organisations have excellent technical facilities and employ highly-qualified teams of experts in their cellars. The quality of their wines is invariably excellent, but usually 'commercial' in character and much the same, year after year. This, however, is not necessarily a bad attribute, but may be somewhat boring to the more adventurous wine drinker.

The Bergkelder, part of the Distillers' group, has partnership arrangements with a score of wine estates to market their wines under estate labels. These products include many prestige names such as Meerlust, Alto, L'Ormarins and Allesverloren.

CO-OPS

Co-operative wineries are established by groups of farmers so that they may make use of a jointly-owned pressing cellar. These employ a winemaker to run the cellar, and most of the wines they produce are sold in bulk to the big and established wholesalers, who use them in their blended, brand-name wines.

Most co-operatives, however, produce a small quantity of their own wines, and these are often excellent value for money. Some co-ops are very small and have only three or four members, while others are vast organisations.

Vredendal Co-op on the West Coast, for example, presses about 50 000 tons of grapes annually. Nuy Co-operative near Worcester, on the other hand, presses only about 9 000 tons. (Nuy, incidentally, is earning an enviable reputation for its superb red and white muscadels, which are said by some to be the best in South Africa.)

At least one co-op, Swartland Co-op in Malmesbury, has decided to market all the wine they produce rather than sell in bulk, and the venture appears to have been very successful.

Co-op wines were once considered to vary in quality and standard, but in recent years the standard of co-op wines has improved considerably, and they regularly win awards at regional and national wine shows.

ESTATES

Estates are the smallest wine-producing units recognised by the KWV, and they make some of the most interesting wines available in the country. Because the estate vineyards and cellar are usually controlled by the same person, wines can be 'designed' with great care and accuracy.

Many wine estates do their own marketing, sometimes selling almost all their wines from the farm. Other estates have wine merchants who do their marketing for them.

PRIVATE PRODUCERS

A recent feature on the Cape wine scene has been the emergence of a few private wine producers, who do not have their own vineyards, but who buy grapes from farms and make their own wine. Probably the most famous is Neil Ellis, who now runs the cellar at Louisvale, near Stellenbosch, making his own wines from the grapes he selects on other farms.

WINE ROUTES

A number of wine routes have been established by wine producers in the main winemaking areas, to enable visitors to buy wine from members' farms and co-operative cellars in the district.

Naturally, the intention is to promote the sale of wines from the area. Brochures are published, with maps of the area and listing the times cellars are open to the public.

Tourism figures released recently show that the wine routes are the second most popular tourist feature of the Cape, closely following Table Mountain.

The best known wine route is in Stellenbosch, which was the first to be established, and has extended its activities to include attractions like farm restaurants, wine museums and hiking trails.

All wine route members offer wine tastings to visitors and, naturally, this is the most pleasant way to buy wines.

There are well-established routes in Paarl, Robertson, Franschhoek, Worcester, Constantia and the West Coast. Details are available from tourist information offices or travel agents.

No visit to the Cape is complete without a day or two in the winelands. There is something special about visiting a wine farm, meeting the winemaker and taking home a case or two of reasonably priced wines from the fellow who made them. Perhaps you could even pick up a few tips from a well-informed insider.

BIRTH OF A BUS TICKET

In order to accurately inform wine consumers about the contents of their wine bottles, the South African wine industry introduced an official control system in 1973. The system laid down a set of standards to be met regarding information on the bottle outlining the origin of the wine.

This 'Wine of Origin' system has worked well and has served its purpose, but is now in the process of being altered to suit the changing times.

There are, however, many bottles of wine on the shelves carrying the now familiar 'bus ticket' on the neck, and these are likely to be around for some years yet.

It is important to remember that the Wine of Origin seal is not a seal of quality, but simply offers some facts about the wine.

Many buyers are under the impression that a two-stripe wine is better than a one-striper, and that a three-stripe wine outranks a two-striper - much like military ranks. This is by no means correct.

Wines submitted for certification (and remember that some of the country's best-known wines are not certified) are examined by a panel of experts, who decide whether the wine is, in fact, what the producer claims it to be.

When the wine has passed a taste test and a chemical analysis, it is awarded a ticket that can have one or more bands, or stripes.

A blue band tells us that the wine originates from a particular area. In other words, although many kinds of grapes may have been used in the wine, all the grapes are from the same area.

The red band states that the wine is a vintage wine. Do not, however, jump to conclusions about the quality of the wine. This does not mean the same as a 'Vintage' wine in France, where the term denotes a particularly good wine season. In South Africa 'vintage' simply means that all the grapes used in that wine were harvested in the same season.

The green band is the cultivar band and means that at least 75% of the wine in the bottle is from the cultivar stated on the label.

Additional information can also be conveyed by the ticket. If, for example, the word 'Estate' appears on the bottle, it means that all the grapes were grown on a single estate (the smallest wine area recognised by the Wine and Spirit Board), even though the wine may have been bottled elsewhere.

If, in the opinion of the panel of tasters, the wine is of superior quality, it is awarded a gold-coloured bus ticket bearing the word 'Superior'.

Even this apparent seal of quality is regarded with some suspicion in certain circles, as the certification board appears to have awarded a large number of Superiors, rather debasing their value.

One of the disadvantages of the Wine of Origin system is that it has, unfortunately, encouraged producers to concentrate on cultivar wines, rather than on blends.

Many of the world's finest wines are the result of skilful blending, and the Wine of Origin system may have caused South Africa to fall behind the rest of the wine world in this respect. The bus tickets, however, will soon be discarded in favour of a more practical and accurate system.

"Then there's the question of organoleptic assessments."

THE TASTING RITUAL

PRACTICAL OR PRETENTIOUS?

It could be said that we taste wine every time we drink it. Certainly, we are aware that it has a flavour.

In this little book, we have taken 'tasting' to mean a careful sensory examination of a wine. This is sometimes known in lofty wine circles as an 'organoleptic assessment' of the wine.

There's always been a certain amount of scoffing about the way wine tasters taste a wine. All the sniffing and spitting and rolling of the eyes seems a little unusual to those who don't know what it's all about. But each step in the wine tasting ritual is intended to serve a real purpose.

Wine comes in many guises, from heavy, tannic reds to cheerful semi-sweet wines for picnics, honey-sweet dessert wines, rich and woody Chardonnays, and the entire range of pink wines, from delicate blancs de noir to pretty pink rosés.

Many fine wines are produced in South Africa every year - each of them unique and interesting. Each wine is the result of a combination of influencing factors, such as the type of grapes used, the soil in which they grew, the season in which they ripened, and both the hand that tended the vine and made the wine.

Wine is made to give pleasure, and the only valid reason for drinking wine is to enjoy it. Anybody who drinks wine for any other reason is a fool. The purpose of tasting wine is to increase your own enjoyment of this wonderful liquid, which is, in a very real sense, a distillation of sunshine.

There are several reasons for going through the traditional tasting ritual. One is simply to become acquainted with a new wine. You taste it properly to find out what sort of wine it is, and how it differs from other wines.

Another reason is to compare various wines, either as part of a competition or simply for interest. A group of wine lovers might like to compare several wines made from the same kind of grape by different winemakers - or to compare wines from the same cellar, made from the same grapes, but in different years.

In a restaurant, a wine is tasted to check whether it meets one's expectations and whether it is in good condition. For this kind of tasting there is a slightly different routine.

RESTAURANT TASTING

The wine waiter should present the unopened bottle to you before drawing the cork. You can then check that it is indeed the wine for which you asked, and feel the bottle to see whether the wine is being served at the correct temperature. When you're satisfied, allow him to draw the cork.

Ideally the wine steward should present the cork to you for inspection before pouring the wine. I have, however, seen this done only two or three times.

A cork is a handy indicator of the wine's condition. If the cork appears crumbly or mouldy, this means that it could have lent a corky flavour to the wine. If the wine has stained the cork along its entire length, there's a possibility that the bottle has been stored in poor conditions and that heat has caused the wine to expand and be forced out past the cork.

Bear in mind, though, that cork is a porous material and if a wine has been maturing in the bottle for some years, you can expect it to have penetrated the cork for some distance.

TASTING

To taste, fill a tasting glass to the widest part of the bulb. Some tasting glasses have a line inscribed at this level for your convenience.

The first step is to hold the glass up to the light. The wine should be brilliantly clear and free of particles (some older wines do, however, contain a deposit of tartrate crystals, but there is no cause for concern).

COLOUR

The colour of the wine can tell the taster a great deal about the wine.

Young white wines often have a greenish tint, while older white wines sometimes develop a golden or amber colour.

Young red wines may be a pinkish purple, while older reds develop a brownish orange colour. The colours are most noticeable at the edge of the pool of wine in your glass, which is why the glass is usually tilted slightly while examining it. This way, the surface of the wine increases and the colour is more clearly observable.

Now swirl the wine around in the glass to release the aroma and bouquet (aroma is the odour of the grape cultivar, while bouquet is the odour that develops in the bottle with maturation). You might like to trap the odours by covering the glass with your free hand while swirling it around.

Hold it up to the nose and take a breath. Does it smell typical of a wine made from that variety of grape? Is it a clean, fresh odour or a stale, musty one? Remember that most of the sensation we know as 'taste' is actually formed by our sense of smell.

Finally, take a mouthful of the wine, roll it round the mouth and breathe in through it. The ritual may sound laughable, but it carries the odours up to the back of the nose.

If you're tasting a large number of wines, it is not necessary to swallow them all. You will probably be provided with a spittoon at such a tasting.

You simply hold the wine in your mouth for a few moments, then spit it into the spittoon.

After tasting the wine, take note of its 'farewell', or aftertaste. This should linger on the palate, so that you may continue to taste the wine long after you've swallowed it.

The taste of some rather dull wines simply vanish after being sipped, leaving no aftertaste at all.

If you're scoring a number of wines, try not to take too long over each one. First impressions may be the most accurate. If you go back to a previous wine and then try to change your opinion of the one you're tasting, your palate is likely to become hopelessly confused.

Taste, close your eyes for a few seconds to experience as much of the wine's character as you can, then jot down your score.

TABOOS

As the sense of smell plays such an important part in tasting wines, strong odours can obviously affect the taste of the wine considerably.

Men should avoid wearing after-shave lotion or cologne, and women should not wear perfume or lipstick during serious tastings (if you're wearing lipstick when tasting a sparkling wine, it will go flat very quickly).

Sometimes wine glasses carry traces of dishwashing liquid, which could affect the tastes of the wines in the glass.

To get rid of this, pour a small amount of wine into it, swirl it around and pour it into the next glass. Repeat the process with each glass and then pour out the wine. This should remove any traces of soap. (You could use water, of course, but tap water often contains traces of chlorine and other purifying chemicals which might add their own characters to the wine.)

Some foods detract from or alter the flavour of a wine drunk soon afterwards. Eggs make a wine taste of sulphur, and fennel and asparagus destroy the flavour. Vinegar dulls the taste of the wine. (If you're going to taste wine after dinner, use lemon juice in a salad dressing, rather than vinegar.)

Although the popular cheese and wine combination goes well together, cheese does tend to dull the palate and is not an appropriate snack to serve at a serious tasting.

Apple, on the other hand, tends to excite the taste-buds and sharpen the palate. There's an old saying that wine merchants should "sell on cheese and buy on apples".

IMPORTANT

Remember that wine tasting is considered an art form by many wine lovers. There are people with amazing taste memories, who are able to sip a wine and identify it.

It is important to remember, however, that this should not be the real object of tasting wines.

Don't be intimidated by people who like to flaunt their knowledge of wine. Wine should never be the cause of embarrassment.

There is only one reason for drinking wine, and that is for enjoyment. If wine tastings can add to your enjoyment, then they have a worthwhile role to play.

THE RIGHT SOCIAL CIRCLE

ESTABLISHING YOUR OWN WINE CIRCLE

The fascinating world of wine can be made even more enjoyable by joining a wine circle or tasting group. After all, pleasures were meant to be shared.

And if there isn't a wine circle in your area, why not start one of your own? A wine circle may be as informal - or as formal - as you would like it to be.

Some groups consist of members who have attended courses and written examinations on wine and enjoy the subject on a rather technical level. Others prefer to simply get together to sample new wines, and share their wine discoveries. They chat about the wines they have tasted and make a few notes so they'll know which wines they would prefer when faced with endless rows of bottles on the store shelves.

Winemakers and wine sellers are usually delighted to address groups of enthusiasts, so it is seldom a problem to obtain a speaker to introduce the wines of the evening.

GETTING STARTED

It really is quite simple. Once you have decided to form a tasting circle or club, simply gather a group of wine enthusiasts eager to participate. The ideal number of members is about 20, because this allows everybody to taste from one bottle of wine. You may decide to have a few more, because there will seldom be a 100% attendance at every meeting.

Having more than 20 members, however, means you may have to find two or more bottles of the wine you want to taste. This is not usually a problem, but could be difficult on some occasions when a member manages to obtain a single bottle of some rare or unusual wine and would like to share it with the group.

"h'mmm"

On the other hand, if you have less than 10 members, winemakers and wine experts might feel it not really worth their while to travel what may be a long way to present an evening of their wines to only a handful of guests. Remember, you will seldom have 100% attendance, so the turnout could be embarrassingly small.

No matter how small or unsophisticated your wine circle may be, you'll need to elect a committee to keep matters running smoothly and efficiently. Don't be tempted to say: "Oh, we'll just keep it informal. We don't need a committee". Do not depend on goodwill and good intentions for a smooth operation. We all know what road is paved with good intentions.

Informal clubs simply fade away. Somebody has to decide when the next meeting is to be held, and where, and who will introduce the wines, and how the costs will be covered. Ideally the membership of the committee should change from time to time to encourage a flow of new ideas.

CONSTITUTION: Even the smallest club must have a written constitution. This, however, need not be a long or complicated document crammed with legal jargon. A sample constitution is included in this book merely as a suggested starting point. Change it to suit your own club or discard it and write your own. But do try to draw up a constitution.

FINANCES: We are not talking about transactions involving thousands of rands, but financial arrangements like: "Oh, we'll all just chip in as much as we need to cover the costs", just don't work.

Probably the best way to begin is to have a small annual subscription and charge a nominal fee or each tasting evening.

The subscriptions should cover the costs of incidental expenses such as stationery, telephone calls and postage, as well as the cost of the first few bottles of wine.

The entrance fees for tastings serve two purposes. They pay for the wines to be tasted at the next meeting, and they ensure that anybody who said they would attend really do. There is nothing more infuriating than arranging a tasting for 25 guests, and then having only 12 people pitch up.

If you're lucky enough to have a winemaker who is willing to supply the wines for a tasting free of charge, still charge your members an entrance fee, and add the money to the kitty.

Let's say you start with 15 members and charge an annual subscription of R10 each. You, therefore, start with R150. I suggest an entrance fee of about R5 for each tasting evening. You'll probably have a dozen members attending, giving you R60. This should be enough to buy you five or six interesting wines for the next tasting.

Some successful wine groups insist on payment before the meeting, when the invitation is accepted. This eliminates the problem of having the treasurer left with unused wines that have to be paid for.

Book-keeping need not be elaborate. All that is required is that the treasurer should keep a list of expenditure and income jotted down in a school exercise book or note book, and open a savings account for the club.

INFORMATION: A minute book, recording the meetings, discussions, the wines tasted and the general opinion of the club members on each wine, could prove interesting.

Once you've established a wine circle, let people in the wine industry know about it. This way, you'll receive a regular flow of literature and advice about new wines.

You could write to the public relations departments of large wine wholesalers like Gilbeys, Stellenbosch Farmers' Winery advising them of the existence of your circle.

Encourage members to have their names included on the mailing lists of established wine cellars and organisations such as the Wine of the Month Club.

It may be a good idea for your circle to subscribe to the KWV publication, *Wynboer*, but draw up a roster to ensure that all the members of the club have a chance to read the articles, which are often very informative.

FORM OF MEETINGS

To be successful, even the most informal club must have some agenda or order of business. If the members simply roll up and start tasting and chatting, the entire evening could degenerate into a booze-up. And, while we have nothing against a good booze-up, we're talking about wine circles here.

Always tackle business first. Decide who is to present the next month's tasting, where it will be held, and when. Discuss details such as the provision of snacks, and whether the club should purchase its own tasting glasses. If you have invited a guest speaker to introduce the wines, make sure somebody is delegated to introduce the guest to the members. It's only polite to do so. And to thank him or her afterwards, of course.

Questions and comments should be introduced in an orderly way, and this is the duty of the chairman.

If you want to retain an informal mood in your tasting circle, appoint a different chairman - or master of ceremonies - for each tasting evening.

TYPES OF TASTINGS

Winemaker's tasting Invite a winemaker to present a selection of his or her wines, discussing each one and explaining why it was made in that particular style.

Cultivar tasting Select a range of wines made from the same grape cultivar - say a Pinotage or Rhine Riesling - and, if possible, from the same vintage. Tastings of this kind are also known as 'horizontal tastings'. This, however, has nothing to do with the proximity of your body to the floor.

Select a member of the club to introduce the wines (maybe the member could do some research on a particular cultivar, where it seems to do best, where it originated, how it got its name and so on). Ask for comments from members. Are the wines different? Are some sweeter than others? Which style seems to be best for that cultivar? Should they be drunk now, or left to mature for a few more years? And so on.

Vintage tasting This type of tasting is occasionally referred to as 'vertical tastings'. Compare and discuss a selection of vintages of the same wine. Are there some good years and some bad ones? Does age improve the wine?

Regional tasting The club could arrange to taste a selection of wines from a particular region or country. Some wine areas employ public relations officers and these people are usually quite happy to present a tasting of wines from their region. Is there any one characteristic common to all the wines from the area? Which cultivars seem to do best in the area?

Personal tasting A club member - or a guest - could present a tasting of some of his or her favourite wines. Maybe they could be special wines from his own cellar, or wines that have very special memories. (It should, of course, be club policy to offer to pay for the wines that are tasted if they're from a private cellar.)

Special occasion tasting Organise a tasting of a few appropriate wines for a particular occasion - French wines for Bastille Day, Californian wines for the Fourth of July, romantic wines for Valentine's Day or sparkling wines for the festive season. Maybe an appropriate celebrity (a writer or French ambassador, a lecturer or a hotel proprietor) could be invited to present the wines.

BLIND TASTINGS

Wine tastings are often conducted 'blind' - which means that the tasters do not know the wine they are tasting.

There is a sound reason for doing this. Many fine and expensive wines have reputations of greatness. A glimpse of the label can actually alter your expectations for that wine. You KNOW in advance that it's good, because of its great reputation. Or you see that it's a very common commercial plonk, so you taste it with a mental scoff. Often the 'great' wines fare quite badly at blind tastings, while some very reasonably priced wines score very well. This is actually good news, because it means there are still many bargains to be found, as long as you're willing to look for them.

A blind tasting can be arranged in several ways. The simplest is for the organiser to place each bottle in an opaque paper bag with just the bottle neck protruding and a number written on the bag for identification. Or the wine can be decanted into numbered carafes or beakers (but make sure they are absolutely clean and do not contain traces of dishwashing liquid, or anything which could affect the taste). Some shops sell tasting bags - numbered bags designed to slip over bottles and conceal their labels.

SCORING

For added interest, issue members with score sheets. These may provide the source for plenty of discussion, and possibly heated debate, but may also be kept as a personal record of the wines tasted.

It always helps to be able to look back and see which wines you awarded high scores - especially when you want to buy some more.

Probably the most common scoring system used in South Africa is to award points out of a total of 20. This is made up of three points for colour and clarity, seven points for nose (aroma and bouquet) and 10 points for flavour and finish (aftertaste, or farewell).

A total of zero to eight points indicates that the wine is poor, and does not warrant you handing over hard-earned money for a product which tastes little better than vinegar. A score of nine or 10 means the wine is below average. An average, but unimpressive wine may score 11 or 12 points and a satisfactory wine would be scored 13 or 14 points. A score of 15 or 16 indicates that you consider the wine very good, and anything from 17 to 20 shows that you consider the wine superior, or excellent. In wine shows, wines that score 17 or more are given gold awards.

A sample score sheet is provided at the end of this chapter. You can have your own printed or find somebody with a photocopying machine and make your own copies.

TASTING COMPETITIONS

Members of a wine circle might enjoy an occasional tasting competition - just for fun. These are not difficult to organise. A selection of about six wines is prepared for a blind tasting as described above. Contestants are provided with tasting glasses and a score sheet and are required to identify the various cultivars, and in some cases, the vintages as well. Some people with good taste memories may even be able to identify the brands of some of the wines.

It may be interesting to test the members' wine memories by using the same wines with which they had been presented in an open tasting. Allow them to taste six wines, knowing what each one is, then have a break of about 15 minutes, and then present the same six in a different order, but this time conceal the labels. See how many they can identify.

Sound easy? Just try it! This is the way the annual SFW Wine Tasting Competition is organised.

REMEMBER - contests like these should never be allowed to become a source of embarrassment. Wine tasting should always be a pleasure, not an embarrassment. If a member gets all six wrong, it really isn't important.

SAMPLE CONSTITUTION

SIPPERS WINE TASTING SOCIETY.

THE AIMS of the club are as follows:
1. To improve the members' knowledge and enjoyment of wine through regular discussions and tastings.
2. To provide closer links, wherever possible, between the producers and distributors of good wines, and those who enjoy them.

MEMBERSHIP shall be limited to not more than 21 members. To become a member of the club, a candidate should be proposed and seconded by two paid-up members, and the proposal accepted by a meeting of the club members. At least 12 members shall be present to constitute a quorum at any meeting.

Members will pay an annual subscription fee, to be determined at the club's annual general meeting, and also an entrance fee to each meeting, to cover the costs incurred for the meeting.

THE COMMITTEE shall be responsible for the smooth running of the club, organising regular meetings and controlling such finances as there may be in the club's account.

The committee, elected at the annual general meeting, shall consist of a chairman, secretary, treasurer and one additional member.

MEETINGS shall be held once a month on the second Wednesday evening of the month, for the purpose of tasting and discussing wines and matters related to wine, its production and enjoyment.

Members will be advised of the meeting venues and times in a monthly notice to be sent by the secretary to each member.

An annual general meeting shall be held in June every year to elect a new committee and to decide on both the subscription fee and meeting fees for the ensuing year, and to discuss any other matters affecting the club.

THE CONSTITUTION shall not be altered without the vote of at least two thirds of the paid-up members.

SIPPERS CLUB TASTING SHEET

TASTER:						DATE:
WINE	VIN-TAGE	COLOUR	NOSE	FLAVOUR	TOTAL	COMMENTS
		3	7	10	20	

"Your main course, Monsieur."

AT YOUR SERVICE

THE PROTOCOL OF SERVING WINE

A lot is said about the correct and incorrect way to serve wine and, with no disrespect to self-styled 'connoisseurs', its all a lot of delightful rubbish. Ideally, the correct way to serve wine is to get it from the bottle to the glass with the least possible spillage, and without knocking over any furniture or collecting any unnecessary dry-cleaning bills at the same time.

A REAL CORKER

The first step is to remove the cork from the bottle (unless it has a screw-cap which, for the uninitiated, you simply twist off).

Corkscrews come in a fascinating variety of shapes and sizes, and most work reasonably well. For the sake of dignity, it is advisable to buy a corkscrew that incorporates some sort of leverage system, otherwise you may end up clutching the bottle between your feet and pulling on the cork with all your might. Not the picture of elegance and serenity.

Very common in South Africa is the type with two arms, which rise as you screw the spiral into the cork. Once the cork is securely impaled, you press down on the arms and the cork is drawn gently from the bottle neck. Some work better than others, so beware of very cheap, shoddy ones.

The corkscrew known as the 'butler's friend' is the more traditional. This incorporates a small knife blade for cutting off the top of the lead or plastic capsule, and a short arm which rests against the lip of the bottle and provides the leverage necessary to remove the cork. The butler's friend is very efficient and has the advantage of folding down into a compact shape that can be slipped into your pocket. Unfortunately, it can just as easily be slipped into a guest's pocket, so they tend to have very short lives. Corkscrews, like the family silver, have a strange allure for petty thieves.

Perhaps the most efficient is the screwpull. The spiral is enclosed between two plastic arms which simply rest on the rim of the bottle once the spiral has been screwed in. To lift the cork, you simply continue to turn the handle, and the cork is twisted out gently and easily. The only disadvantage is that they tend to be rather expensive.

Another type of cork puller has two slender blades, rather than a spiral screw. The blades are slipped carefully down the sides of the cork and rotated to withdraw the cork undamaged. The better ones work well, but it does seem rather a bother, when a good corkscrew does the job just as well. There is, after all, no market for undamaged wine corks.

When buying a corkscrew, carefully examine the actual spiral screw. Some cheap models simply munch up the cork, leaving an irritating handful of crumbs and a cork damaged beyond recognition, but still lodged firmly in the bottle neck. If you own one of these, throw it away immediately. There's no need for the pleasure of drinking wine to be preceded by a violent confrontation with the bottle and its cork.

Corkscrews with an open thread, like a spiral of wire, seldom damage the cork.

The kind of cork-removing gadget that works on air pressure and has a long hypodermic needle to push through the cork, and a pump to fill the bottle with air, should be avoided. It's a silly gimmick and can cause the bottle to explode if there's a flaw in the glass.

BANGS AND BUBBLES

There is a simple way of removing the cork from a bottle of sparkling wine or Champagne. Wine waiters often get it wrong. Racing drivers never get it right.

Presumably the idea of opening a bottle of sparkling wine is to drink the stuff, not spray it about. So it is best not to pop the cork into the air and then make a desperate grab for the nearest glass to catch as much of the fountain as you can.

Make sure that the bottle has not been shaken. Remove the capsule (these sometimes have a little red tag, which can be pulled to tear the capsule at a convenient place).

Twist the wire ring to open it, and remove the wire cage from the cork. Now, holding the cork firmly in your left hand and the bottle firmly in your right hand, remove the bottle from the cork (rather than the cork from the bottle) by twisting and pulling it downwards. You should hear a small pop and the cork will stay in your left hand, landing in nobody's soup and causing nobody to be hospitalised for emergency surgery.

TEMPERATURE

Now THIS is where controversy reigns supreme!

White wines, we are repeatedly informed, should be served chilled, while red wines should be served at 'room temperature'.

But remember that this rule was made before the introduction of air conditioning and central heating. In those days red wine was probably a favourite drink to warm the cockles of the heart during the European winter, when homes were draughty and chilly.

But can you apply the same rule to a Durban living room in December? The concept makes no sense at all. What really matters is that we drink our wines as we like them. In summer a chilled glass of dry white wine is very refreshing. But nobody wants a glass of tepid red wine. If you prefer red wine, rather pop it into the fridge for an hour or two before you open it.

And if it's a chilly Highveld evening and the red wine comes to the table almost frozen, stand it in a bucket of lukewarm water for a few minutes to take off the chill.

There are people who demand that their wine be served at a precise temperature. Although this practice may be a little pretentious, appropriate temperatures for certains wines have been established. If you insist on knowing the 'ideal' temperatures for serving wines, whites are usually best at between eight and 10 degrees celsius and reds at about 15 degrees celsius. It really is as simple as that.

Remember that sherries, jerepigos and noble late harvests are also best when slightly chilled.

But it's your wine, and you can do whatever you please with it. (The purists will shudder at the thought of adding ice to wine, but a really delightful summer drink can be made by pouring a rich, sweet muscadel over a glass of crushed ice. Try it.)

Wine stores and gift shops sell expensive little wine thermometers, usually in hand-crafted wooden cases, designed more for giving than for using. These are ideal if you enjoy playing wine games, or if you simply don't know WHAT to give Uncle George for Christmas, but they serve no real purpose.

Next time you see a wine thermometer, check whether 'room temperature' is marked anywhere on the dial, and then check this against the temperature of the room if you really have nothing better to do with your time.

If you want to know the temperature of a bottle of wine, simply feel it with your hand. Unless you have leprosy, you'll be able to tell whether it is chilled or warm. That's how mothers have tested babies' bottles for centuries and it has always worked.

RESTAURANT TRAUMAS

For some strange reason, many people feel threatened by the prospect of ordering wine in a restaurant. By comic-book tradition, wine waiters are a snooty bunch, but there is no need to settle for coffee or tea when what you really want is a bottle of wine.

Fortunately, the archetypal 'nose-in-the-air' wine steward is rare in South Africa.

The first step when ordering wine in a restaurant is to study the wine list. Take your time and don't panic.

If it is a good wine list it will contain some basic information about each wine - whether it is red or white, sweet or dry, heavy or light-bodied and so on. The very least it should do is categorise the wine under 'Red' or 'White'.

Most restaurants offer a few reasonably-priced 'house wines' as well as many very expensive, fancy wines and probably some imported ones at more than fancy prices.

The wine waiter will possibly recommend one of the more expensive wines, but that's his job. Remember that the restaurant is there to make money.

You, on the other hand, are there to enjoy an evening of fine wining and dining - preferably without worrying about how to face your bank manager the following day.

There's no stigma attached to ordering a house wine, and it is unlikely to be a bad one. It was, after all, specially selected by the restaurateur for his patrons.

Ask the diners at your table what they will be ordering, and select a wine that seems to go with most of the selections.

In this case, it may be safer to stick to the 'red wine with red meat' rule, unless everybody prefers white. If there's a strong division of tastes, and if you can afford it, order a red and a white wine.

When you've ordered the wine, the waiter should bring the unopened bottle to you. This is to enable you to check that it is, in fact, what you ordered, and to feel whether it is at an acceptable temperature. When you're satisfied, tell him to go ahead and open the bottle.

Ideally, he should show you the cork, so you can see that it is not mouldy or rotten. This, however, is a rare courtesy even at the smartest eateries, and hardly worth making a fuss about - unless you want to impress pretentious friends or humiliate the smug waiter.

Before he proceeds to fill the glasses of your guests the waiter should first pour a little wine into your glass for you to taste.

Hold the glass up to the light to check that it's clear and has no solids suspended in it. If the wine looks cloudy, expect something to be wrong. Fortunately, today's wines are rarely faulty. Swirl it around once or twice to release some of the aroma, and sniff the wine. It should not smell like mouldy cork. If it smells reasonably pleasant, take a sip and swish it about in your mouth for a moment to taste it.

It is not acceptable to spit in a restaurant. Most patrons prefer not to be reminded of that particular cultural ritual when they are somewhere between hors d'oeuvres and dessert.

If the wine is sound, allow the waiter to pour for the rest of the guests. The correct order is to start with the women and then the men, pouring from behind the right shoulder of each guest, in order to disrupt the dining as little as possible.

That's really all there is to it.

If you do happen to feel unhappy about the wine, it might be diplomatic to call the maître d'hôtel and to ask for his opinion. Shouting verbal abuse at the dumb-struck waiter and loudly refusing to pay the bill is not going to endear you to your guests or the other patrons. Consulting the maître d'hôtel makes him feel important too, and implies that you respect his judgement in wine matters - always a flattering gesture.

He probably drinks whisky, anyway.

STOP IT!

Just as there are many untruths about wine, there are just as many about corks. All the best wines, we are told, are sealed with corks. Only inferior wines are sold in bottles with screw-caps.

"Frankly, my dear chap, I wouldn't use any other corkscrew."

This may be the case, but it certainly isn't the cork that makes the wine good, or the screw-cap that makes it bad. Logically, the cork is there simply to ensure that the wine does not spill from the bottle until it is required.

Cork was originally used for sealing bottles because there were no alternatives available at the time. The bark of the cork oak has a springy, closed-cell structure that allows it to be squeezed up tightly and return to more or less its original shape. It also doesn't absorb moisture readily (which is why it is used in life-rings on ships.)

But many wine producers say cork is by no means the ideal wine bottle closure. It's very expensive, and inferior corks tend to rot, or to absorb wine. Being a natural product, quality varies from one cork to the next. Some corks leak. And if they're allowed to dry, they shrink and let air into the bottle, ruining the wine. This is why we store wine bottles on their sides, to keep the corks wet.

A modern screw-cap eliminates all these problems.

So why are corks still used for the best wines?

The answer is that there's more to wine than just taste.

CIRCUMSTANCE AND CEREMONY

Wine drinking is a complete experience. It includes the company, the discussion, the surroundings, the elegant glassware and, of course, the ritual of pulling the cork.

Just as a pipe smoker will have his favourite tobacco jar, pipe and smoking accessories, so wine lovers have their favourite corkscrews.

And the anticipation of a really fine wine is heightened by the careful cutting of the lead capsule, the insertion of the corkscrew point, the twisting, the pulling, the soft 'pop' as the cork is drawn.

Then there's that moment of doubt as the cork is examined. Is it sound? Has the wine survived?

Spin off a screw-cap and all that is lost. You know the wine's going to be OK. Nothing ever goes wrong with a screw-cap. But where's the ROMANCE?

Seriously, though, several Cape wine farmers have experimented recently with bottling identical wines in corked bottles as well as screw-capped bottles. So far there has been no indication that the corked bottles are any better. Or any worse.

At Simonsvlei Co-op they offer a choice of corks or screw-caps for some of their wines. The screw-caps are slightly cheaper than the corks, but some customers still prefer corks. They simply have a more 'classy' aura about them.

If you find a wine you enjoy, and it's sealed with a screw-cap, go for it. There should be no social stigma attached to a screw-capped wine. Remember that some of the world's most expensive whiskies and cognacs are sealed with screw-caps. Nothing cheap and nasty about THEM!

On the other hand, don't mock the ritual of cork-pulling either. The presentation of any pleasure is an important part of it. It's all very well to simply throw a fine piece of jewellery into a woman's lap and say: "Catch! There's a present for you". It's another matter if the gift is prettily wrapped, tied with an elegant bow and presented at a candle-lit dinner. Now that's romance.

PS. AND while we're on the subject of presentation and the total experience of wine drinking, it may be appropriate to consider the matter of blind tastings.

Can we do justice to a wine by sniffing it and tasting it in the cold, clinical atmosphere of a laboratory or tasting room? When we select an old bottle of fine red wine from a good cellar, we approach it with anticipation - almost with reverence. We are prepared to give it our full attention. We open it with care and serve it in the best glass we can find, because such a wine is far too good for a plastic mug or a cheap tumbler.

We enjoy the anticipation of sharing this treasure with good friends. And of course the experience is a memorable one - the whole experience, not just the wine. "Ah, remember that superb bottle of 1972 Cabernet we drank with Joe and Wendy? Wonderful evening!" That same wine might pass almost unnoticed in a blind tasting held in a laboratory. "Not bad. Give it 15 out of 20. Next!"

In a recent experiment, six wine tasters were offered a selection of wines in a blind tasting in a laboratory setting. They scored them and their scores were noted.

Some weeks later, unknown to the tasters, they were offered the same wines, again in a blind tasting, but this time in the elegant setting of an up-market hotel reception room at a prestige wine event.

In every case, their scores were higher than they had been in a cold clinical laboratory.

Wine is never just a matter of flavour.

WINE AND THE GLASS

SERVING WINE IN THE CORRECT GLASS

Phyllis Hands, who runs the Cape Wine Academy in Stellenbosch, has a simple rule about wine glasses. "They mustn't leak," she says.

After all, the only real function of the wine glass is to transfer the wine comfortably from the bottle to your mouth.

Anybody who holds definite ideas about the 'correct' glass for a Burgundy or a white wine is simply being pretentious. Drinking wine should be a complete experience, engaging all the senses, so an elegant glass obviously gives more satisfaction than a clumsy, misshapen one. The form, fineness and transparency of a glass may add much to the savouring of a wine.

A clear crystal glass allows you to appreciate the colour of the wine, but a green- or blue-coloured glass, or an elegantly crafted silver goblet may have a charm of its own.

Personally, I think metal goblets may be well suited to Shakespearean dramas, but I prefer to drink out of glass. I think metal gives the wine a metallic flavour and feels tinny against the teeth, but that's a purely personal foible.

TRADITION RULES

There are, of course, traditional glasses to be used for the various kinds of wine, but this is just tradition - not a law which should be adhered to at all costs.

In fact, I have a sneaking suspicion that the idea of having a different glass for every wine is a clever marketing ploy devised by the manufacturers of glassware.

Champagne, for example, is often depicted being drunk from a wide-mouthed goblet shaped rather like a saucer on a stem. Tradition has it that this glass was modelled to fit Marie Antoinette's breast - a romantic idea, but not particularly practical (or comfortable, I should imagine). One must assume that most people drink sparkling

"sniff, sniff."

wine because they enjoy the bubbles, and the wide-mouthed glass destroys the bubbles. It provides too large a surface area for sparkling wine, and the bubbles are lost very quickly.

Besides, just try wandering about at a party clutching a great saucer of Champagne, and see how far you get without spilling most of it on the other guests. (On the other hand, "Oops" does make for an original opening line - especially if you've been longing to strike up a conversation.)

The tall and elegantly fluted glass is far better suited to sparkling wine. You can see the tiny bubbles rising prettily up the length of the glass and the small surface area allows the wine to keep sparkling for a long time.

For most occasions, a simple, unadorned wine glass is best, regardless of whether you're drinking red or white wine. Ideally, the rim of the glass should be curved slightly inward, as with the tasting glass, to concentrate the aroma. The glass should be thin and clear to allow the drinker to see the colour and clarity of the wine. Heavy or coloured glasses may detract from this.

Traditionally, the wine glass has a stem, so you can lift it without warming the wine with your hands. The bulb should be big enough to hold a decent amount of wine when about two-thirds filled. (A wine glass should never be filled to the brim. If it's too full, you're more likely to spill, and you can't swirl it about to release the aroma.)

Because wine glasses are ideally thin and delicate, they break. It is therefore sensible to choose glasses that are easily replaced, and to buy a few more than you're likely to need.

Traditionally, red wine is served in a slightly larger glass than white wine. The so-called 'Paris Goblet' often used for red wine has a well-rounded bowl, shaped rather like a ball with the top sliced off. This is usually used for full-bodied red wines.

White wine is rather more acidic than red, and is traditionally drunk in smaller quantities, so it is often served in smaller glasses.

This, however, is purely a matter of taste and there is no reason why you shouldn't drink white wine from a vase if it pleases you.

Fortified wines, such as sherry, port, Muscadels and jerepigos, are high in alcohol, and are usually served in very small glasses. The traditional glass used in Spain for sherry, port and Madeira, is called the 'copita' or little cup. The bowl is shaped like a small cylinder and made of thin, clear glass to highlight the colour and clarity of the wine, and allow the brilliance to shine through.

THE GLASS

There's a standard glass used for formal tastings, and it is designed simply to provide the maximum information about the wine.

The bowl of the glass is wide to provide a large surface area from which the volatile odours can escape. The mouth is narrower, so that the odours are concentrated where they can easily be sniffed.

The wine glass is thin and clear, so that the colour and clarity of the wine may easily be observed.

The stem allows the taster to hold the glass to the light without covering the contents with his or her fingers.

SOAP AND WATER

Wine glasses, and especially tasting glasses, must be kept clean if they are to display the colour and brilliance of the wine. For really sparkling glasses, the secret lies in the rinsing and polishing. It's a good idea to wash wine glasses by hand, rather than by dishwasher. It takes only a few seconds to do it properly.

To prevent breakage or scratching, it might be sensible to wash your glasses in a plastic bowl or to first line your sink with a dishcloth. Hard water tends to cloud the glass, so if you live in an area where the water is hard, try adding a little borax.

Immerse the glasses in warm (not hot) soapy water, then rinse them in pure water, leaving a little warm water in the bottom of each glass after rinsing. This is to keep the glass warm, because a warm glass is easier to polish than a cold one.

The glass should be dried and polished with a clean, lint-free dishcloth. Stuff some of the cloth into the bowl of the glass and wrap the rest round the outside. Now grip the foot of the glass and rotate it. Don't grip it too tightly with either hand, or the stem might snap.

Wine glasses should also be given a light polish before they are set on the table. This ensures that there are no fingerprints on them, so they'll be sparkling clear for the drinkers.

STORAGE

Avoid storing wine glasses upside down on a shelf. Glasses stored like this can develop a smell from the paint or coating of the shelf, and can also draw up moisture and become cloudy.

To protect glasses stored upright from gathering dust, simply place a sheet of thin paper over them.

Wine glasses that have been hung from an overhead rack, such as those used in bars, should also be polished before use, as they can pick up room odours or smoke odours.

DECANTERS

Wine buffs can talk all night about whether or not to decant wine. In most cases, the original reason for decanting wine has fallen away.

Old wines usually developed crystals of tartrate at the bottom of the bottle (or the side if it was stored correctly) after a few years in storage. To rid the wine of these crystals the bottle was lifted very gently from the rack, the cork pulled very carefully without disturbing the crystals, and the wine poured slowly into a decanter, leaving the sediment behind in the bottle.

Modern wines are usually stabilised, and do not form tartrate crystals, so there's no real need to decant them. Besides, tartrate crystals are not harmful in any way and the only discomfort they may cause is that they may feel a bit gritty between your teeth, but that's all.

A decanter does, however, look quite attractive on an elegant table setting, and it can be fun to fill a decanter with cheap plonk and test your more pretentious wine friends.

Usually, however, wine lovers like to examine the bottle to know what they're drinking, when it was bottled and so on.

Cut-glass decanters are usually reserved for sherries, spirits and ports, while wine looks better in a clear glass decanter.

"It was a cold and stormy night...
and my throat was dry."

CUPBOARDS AND CORNERS

HANDLING AND STORING YOUR WINE

As an 'ordinary' wine drinker, probably without a cellar, should you bother about laying down red wines?

Remember that we are concerned only with the ENJOYMENT of wines. And to appreciate good red wines at their finest, they should be allowed to age for some years before they are consumed.

If you're very wealthy, you can probably buy good wine already aged in ideal conditions by one of the big wine companies.

It is, however, an expensive way to obtain good wines. No company is going to keep thousands of bottles of red wine in costly air-conditioned maturation cellars unless they can charge customers for the service. That's why aged wines are so expensive.

It is much more fun - and costs far less money - to mature your own red wines.

Two main questions arise - where to store the wine, and what wines to select for maturation.

STORAGE

Ideally, wines should be kept in a cool cellar with a constant temperature of around 15 degrees celsius. Because not many of us can provide ideal storage conditions, alternative storage has to be considered.

The main feature of a cellar at home is not that it should be cold, but rather that the temperature remain constant. Wine - like any liquid - expands when its temperature rises, and contracts when it cools. In a fluctuating temperature, this expansion forces the wine to escape past the cork. When the temperature drops, the wine contracts and may draw a small quantity of air past the cork and into the bottle. Eventually the unwanted air that has been drawn into the bottle oxidises the wine, giving it an unpleasant, 'burnt' flavour, and probably a prematurely brown colour.

If you don't have a proper cellar, try to select a storage place away from a sunny outside wall that gets warm during the day.

Maybe there's a cool place under the stairs, or in a corner of the garage. If you use a cupboard, perhaps you could insulate it by sticking sheets of styrofoam to the sides and doors.

If you live near an airport or a busy street, where heavy traffic passes your home regularly, try to make sure that your wines are kept as stable as possible. Regular movement could disturb the lees, allowing it to mix with the wine and turn your fine wine into vinegar!

Also remember to keep your cellar as clean as possible. Mice and rats are rather fond of dark and quiet places and wine is particularly susceptible to odours. Storing fruit and vegetables alongside your Cabernet would not only attract vermin, but rotting onions, turnips and cabbage could not enhance the bouquet of your wines in any way. Neither would petrol, oil or any other strong-smelling products you might be tempted to store alongside your wine.

WHAT WINE TO LAY DOWN

Not all red wines are intended for long maturation. Many wine-makers find it more profitable to make light-bodied, fresh red wines that can be consumed immediately.

It certainly makes economic sense to be able to sell your wine as quickly as possible.

But there are few pleasures to match the flavour of a rich, well-aged Cabernet or Bordeaux-style red wine that has been properly stored for many years.

When selecting a wine to lay down, remember that it must be able to last a good few years without spoiling, and there are several substances that act as preservatives.

Alcohol is a good preservative, so the wine should have quite a high alcohol content. Tannin is another good preservative and assures a long life. Many young reds have a substantial amount of tannin. This is the astringent substance that puckers the inside of your mouth when you taste the wine. Residual sugar is another preserving agent.

So, when you're selecting a wine to be aged, try to distinguish between the harsh preservatives and the real character of the wine. Under the tannin and raw alcoholic flavours of a young wine, you should be able to taste the fruitiness of the grapes. When all of these components are present, you can be reasonably sure the wine will last a long time and develop into an elegant and smooth drink.

And you can look forward to a really superb wine, knowing that you bought it for a fraction of what it may be worth someday.

Fortified wines can also be rewarding to mature. Their chief preservative is the alcohol which is added to stop fermentation.

When the alcohol is added to the young wine, it does not 'marry' with the wine immediately, but remains rather harsh and separate from the flavour of the wine. In time, however, it becomes part of the smooth character of the wine.

Old jerepigos and muscadels are superb and it is well worth laying down a few bottles of young fortified wine if you have the space.

It is interesting to note that ruby port, however, is not made to be laid down. If it is, it is likely to deposit a heavy sediment in the bottle and lose much of its body.

In tawny ports this sediment is usually deposited in the casks before the wine is bottled, so additional maturation may well improve them.

Most of our white wines are made for drinking young, and South Africans have become used to this style of wine. There are however, several fuller-bodied white wines on the market now, and these will definitely benefit from a few years of maturation.

Look for wooded whites, or white wines with a very rich, mouth-filling flavour and plenty of acidity with the fruitiness. Many Chardonnays and Sauvignon Blancs, in particular, will improve with some bottle maturation.

IT'S A RECORD!

It may seem a little pretentious to keep a 'Wine Diary', but it really is a sensible idea if you want to get the most from your wine.

Not many people have perfect wine memories. Most of us taste a wine and say: "Hey, that's really good", but when we try to remember its name three weeks later at the liquor store, the name has completely slipped our minds.

A wine diary doesn't have to be a venerable, leather-bound tome chained to the cellar table. It can be a simple school exercise book or a note book. All the book needs to be is a record of what wine you tasted, and how you enjoyed it. You need to know whether to buy the same again, or whether the remainder of your stocks of that wine should be drunk immediately or left to mature a little longer.

Of course, you could make a social event of your record keeping, and add the names of the people who shared the wine with you, and some of their comments.

It may be interesting to jot down the food that accompanied the wine, and whether it was a happy combination of flavours.

It could be very useful to be able to say: "I wonder what wine to serve with the chicken casserole tonight. I'll see what we had last time we had chicken casserole." Having a convenient reference, compiled by you according to your own tastes, could make matters so much easier.

The idea behind enjoying your wine is that it should not become a grand and snobbish production. If every bottle of wine you drink entails half an hour of book-keeping, drinking wine is going to be a dreadful chore.

MAKING MEMORIES

It would be far more convenient to have a notebook lying on the shelf with the wine bottles, and to simply jot down the date and: '1984 Pofadder Cabernet for Sam's birthday party'.

Later in the evening, if you feel that there are further notes you would like to make for future reference, you can add: 'Great wine. Went well with the roast squirrel'.

There are, however, many wine lovers who enjoy keeping detailed records and returning to them like holiday-makers return to their snap albums.

Somes wines are not worth recording, but most of us encounter interesting wines from time to time, and would like to keep a record of these.

At least one wine lover we know likes to keep the wine bottles from memorable occasions, and steam off the labels to keep as a record. He then jots down details of the wine and the occasion on the back of the label and collects them. The result is a fascinating combination of memories and information.

Design a record-keeping system that suits you, bearing in mind that it should not be an irritating chore to complete, and it should be useful for future buying - or even for future reminiscing. But if record-keeping ever threatens to spoil your enjoyment of wine, stop immediately and leave the memory-making to your palate.

IN THE KITCHEN

COOKING WITH WINE

Wine has always been as much at home in the kitchen as in the dining room and living room.

Wine is an excellent seasoning for all kinds of food, and can add as much extra flavour as herbs and spices.

As with any seasoning, the quantities are not rigidly laid down. When cooking with wine, be discreet. Wine should subtly enhance and improve your food, so try not to 'drown' the meat - it's already dead. A good cook will know instinctively just how much to add to a particular dish, and some cooks are better than others.

Bear in mind, though, that 'cooking wine' should never be inferior leftovers, especially if you are serving your boss or your bank manager! Poor wines will simply overpower the flavour of dishes you might have spent hours preparing. As with any dish you create, the better the ingredients, the better the final result.

If a wine is not good enough to drink, it certainly isn't good enough to cook with.

If you do happen to have some good leftover wine (but if it's so good, why was it left over?) that you'd like to keep handy in the kitchen, add a teaspoon of sunflower oil to the bottle, and then re-cork it.

The oil will float on the surface and prevent air getting to the wine and oxidising it. But it's still best to taste it before you use it, just to make sure it hasn't turned sour and vinegary. If you want a vinegary taste, try using vinegar.

The invention of the bag-in-a-box has been a boon to the modern cook. The container keeps wine fresh for a very long time, because the foil bag collapses slowly as is it emptied, ensuring that no air reaches the wine.

The handy tap makes it easy for the cook to draw off half a cup of wine, or two tablespoons, as required, without having to agonize about whether to open a new bottle.

"Coq au vin"

THAT LITTLE EXTRA

There's hardly a dish that can't be given extra zest by adding a splash of wine. A good general rule is that wherever the recipe calls for water, milk or stock, you can replace some of it with wine.

Even a packet of instant soup tastes better if a little of the water is replaced by sherry. Sherry has, in fact, become very popular in the kitchen. If you're cooking with raisins or sultanas, try soaking them in a little dry sherry first. The wrinkled fruit will become plump and juicy, and impart a heavenly flavour to your dish.

Add a dash of white wine to a salad dressing to lift it out of the ordinary, or try sprinkling a little wine over boiled potatoes while they're still hot, then let them cool and use them in a potato salad.

A hot wine and cheese topping poured over toast makes a delightful and unusual snack.

You could even add a little white wine to glazed carrots.

Try poaching large, fresh mushrooms in semi-sweet white wine, or pot-roast a chicken in half a bottle of Hanepoot jerepigo.

Freshly collected mussels are delicious poached in an off-dry white wine. You could hardly find an easier recipe than that.

You can even make a delicious wine bread. Just take two cups of self-raising flour and add a teaspoon of salt and two tablespoons of cooking oil. Add enough dry white wine to make a firm dough, and roll it into thin pancake shapes on a floured board. Bake them in a flat-bottomed cast-iron pot, preferably over an open fire.

These are just a few of the ways in which wine can add excitement to your cooking. The list is endless.

The general rule of matching red wine with red meat and white wine with white meat still applies. A gutsy red wine adds a hearty touch to a good stew or roast, and a splash of semi-sweet white wine gives a delicate tang to a chicken or fish dish.

Don't be too concerned about alcohol levels as the heat from your stove or the fire soon causes much of the alcohol to evaporate, leaving only the flavour of the wine behind.

SWEET NOTHINGS

Sweet fortified wines can be incorporated very happily in puddings. Indeed, all you need to round off a meal is a helping of ice-cream with a measure of sweet Hanepoot or Muscadel poured over it.

Or try a can of pears, drained and left to marinate in port or a special late harvest wine for a day or two. (You can add a tot of *witblits* for a rollicking end to the meal, but don't say I told you to do so. It's rather an uncouth thing to do, unless you're on very friendly terms with your dinner guests and don't mind them becoming breakfast guests as well.) We're very lucky to have good cheap wines available in South Africa, so experiment to your heart's content. Wine is for fun.

HOT SIPS

While we're in the kitchen, remember that wine can form the basis for an entire range of warming winter evening drinks. These wine punches are known by various names in various parts of the world. The Norwegians call theirs *glügg*, the British have their 'mulled wine' and the Germans their *gluhwein*.

You can buy ready-mixed sachets of *gluhwein* spices if you're lazy. All you need to do is warm a bottle of red wine in a saucepan, add the sachet and leave it to draw for a while, like a tea-bag. Don't let it boil if you can help it, or all the alcohol will evaporate.

Purists might prefer to make their own *gluhwein* from the traditional recipes. It's an exciting way to brighten an otherwise dull winter evening, and the aroma is usually quite tantalising.

Here's a fairly basic recipe from which to start.

GLUHWEIN
Two cups of boiling water
One cup of brown sugar
Juice of half a lemon
Three sticks of cinnamon
Three whole cloves
Half a teaspoon of grated nutmeg
A bottle of medium-bodied red wine

Combine all the ingredients except the wine in a saucepan and bring it to the boil, stirring occasionally. When the sugar has dissolved, add the wine, and simmer gently, taking care that the mixture does not reach boiling point.

Strain the *gluhwein* into a large jug, and serve in coffee mugs, with a pinch of grated nutmeg over each serving.

FRUITY

Wine is a fruit juice, so it combines rather well with other fruit juices to make all sorts of exciting drinks. Try mixing equal quantities of dry white wine and pineapple juice, with a little ground cinnamon and cloves for flavour, and some sugar to taste. Heat it, but do not allow it to boil, and serve piping hot.

You can do the same with apple juice, but rather use a special late harvest wine instead of the dry white. For that extra sting, add a squeeze of lemon juice before serving.

SANGRIA

The Italian drink, *sangria*, is really just a mixture of orange juice and red wine, but most people have their own variations and individual touches. I like to add a teaspoon of brown sugar to every glass, but others may not have such a sweet tooth. Float a slice of orange on the drink to give your *sangria* that added touch.

Sangria is usually served chilled and in glasses with sugar frosted rims. To frost the glasses, simply dip the rims in a shallow dish of lemon juice and then into a saucer of white sugar. Leave the glasses to dry for a while before serving.

Sangria makes a very refreshing summer drink, and has the advantage of not being too alcoholic, so it's fine for a business lunch.

FIZZ

Just in case the idea of mixing red wine and orange juice distresses you, remember that Champagne and orange juice (sometimes called Buck's Fizz) has been an old favourite for festive breakfasts for ages.

In fact , it's about the ONLY socially acceptable breakfast cocktail I know, and won't leave you light-headed for the rest of the morning.

SPRITZERS

Wine on its own is not a particularly satisfying thirst quencher. In fact, it may aggravate your thirst (which makes the wine sellers very happy, of course). But wine is the base for an excellent thirst quencher, the spritzer.

The spritzer is simply a mixture of white wine and soda water. For a real thirst stopper, use a dry white wine, but if you have a sweet tooth, by all means use a semi-sweet wine. A twist of lemon adds zest to your spritzer.

"Bon appétit".

FORBIDDEN FRUIT

A variation of the spritzer is port and lemonade, which was the very first alcoholic drink I ever tasted as a teenager. Alfred, the wine waiter at the old Central Hotel in Colesberg, took great pride in his 'Port-and-lemon', served with ice and a twist of lemon peel.

My parents, however, seemed rather shocked to learn what I was drinking, and told me that only prostitutes drank port and lemon. In spite of that, or maybe even because of it, I have always enjoyed port and lemon.

MUSCADEL FRAPPÉ

Another wonderful summer drink I discovered in Robertson, where they really KNOW about sweet, fortified wines, is red muscadel poured over a tall glass of crushed ice. Delicious. Try it some time.

THE WAISTLINE

Nutritionists are quick to condemn wine for its alcoholic content, but they also conveniently forget to mention the nourishing action of its mineral salt, iron and vitamin B content.

Several cellars produce so-called 'light' wines in an attempt to catch the slimmers' market. The idea is to produce a wine low in alcohol and sugar, but still full of flavour. Clearly this is impossible, but it gives market-conscious winemakers something to aim for.

If slimming is number one on your list of priorities, however, it may be a good idea to simply cut down on fat and sugar wherever possible. Despite what dieticians may say, you do not necessarily have to do without your regular glass of wine in the evening. Most wines, in fact, are lower in carbohydrates than dietary regulars such as All-Bran flakes and yoghurt, and have fewer calories than margarine and most dried fruit.

If you're still a little hesitant about having wine with your meal, serve wine only with your main course. Most people who are conscious about their weight serve salads and fruits as starters and desserts and these may be too acid to be accompanied by a wine.

If, however, you drink too much wine which contains 'empty' calories, your body will try to compensate by demanding more food. THIS is when the waistline will begin to bulge!

Drinking wine is a social pleasure and only becomes a problem when it is taken in excess, and is accompanied by unbalanced eating habits and an unhealthy lifestyle. Moderation in the pursuit of the finer pleasures of life, however, is by no means a vice.

It may be helpful to remember that food, even party snacks and titbits, helps slow down the rate of alcohol absorption by the body. Proteins also stimulate the liver to release an enzyme which quickly metabolizes alcohol.

It also helps if you drink your wine slowly, remembering that wine is meant to be sipped and savoured, not gulped down like water.

So, wine lovers, there is no need to sacrifice your moderate glass of dry white wine for a tumbler of carrot juice. Simply concentrate on your wine; your waistline isn't going anywhere.

WINNING PARTNERS

There is no other drink that complements a good meal as well as a glass of the right wine. Much has been said about the appropriate wine to serve with a particular dish. The old rule, however, that red wine should be served with red meat and white wine with white meat is merely a useful guide, and not a rigid law.

The reason for the rule is very simple. Red meats, such as beef and venison, are usually full of robust flavour. Most diners feel that this needs a robustly-flavoured wine and the appropriate wines are usually the full-bodied reds.

But there are, of course, exceptions. Many of today's wood-matured Chardonnays and Sauvignon Blancs are quite powerful enough to be enjoyed with roast beef.

If you are to enjoy a meal to the full, every part of that meal should give you pleasure. Serve a gently-flavoured light white wine with a spicy curry, and you're not likely to taste the wine at all. Serve a full-bodied Cabernet Sauvignon with a lightly steamed fish dish, and you won't taste the fish.

Port is traditionally served with cheese after a meal, but there are some delicately flavoured cheeses, like Gouda, which will simply be overwhelmed by a good, rich port. The trick is to find the right balance of flavour between the wine and food.

A GOOD MATCH

Here are some suggestions for matching food and wine. They are offered merely as guides, because most dishes - a stew for example

- can be made in a wide variety of styles and flavours, each of which can be matched with a different wine. Obviously it is impossible to list a wine for every possible dish, so the list given here is merely an idea from which to build your own repertoire. Be creative, and jot down your own successful combinations for future reference.

Roast beef or lamb - A well-matured red wine. Cabernet would be perfect.

Barbecued beef or mutton - An unpretentious red wine. Try a Cinsaut-based blend. Local favourite, 'Tassies' is a good braai wine.

Meat-balls or savoury mince dishes - An ordinary 'house' red wine would go down well.

Roast chicken - A dry white wine would probably be safe, but if it's a particularly flavourful chicken, try a red wine or a dry rosé.

Chinese food - Chinese dishes are often a combination of sweet and savoury flavours, so a semi-sweet white wine is usually ideal. Try a Gewürztraminer or an off-dry Chenin Blanc.

Crayfish - Chardonnay or wooded Sauvignon Blanc.

Curry - Opinions vary. Some people enjoy a dry sparkling wine with curry. A sweet, fortified wine, like a Hanepoot jerepigo, also goes well with a curry, and is strong enough to stand the competition. A special late harvest could also complement a mild curry.

Pizzas - A full-bodied red wine often goes well with a pizza, but if the flavour is not very strong, a rosé or blanc de noir would do.

Pork - Try a Weisser Riesling or a dry blanc de Noir.

Puddings - A sweet, fortified Hanepoot - or even a noble late harvest - would be a good choice.

Soup - A dry sherry is usually served with soup, but a Chardonnay might go well with a thick creamy soup, while a fish soup could call for a crisp dry white wine.

Fish - Tasty fish like kingklip, smoked salmon or sole served in sauce may require a Chardonnay or a wood-matured Sauvignon Blanc. Delicately flavoured fish will probably taste best served with a light, dry Chenin Blanc or South African Riesling.

Breakfast - Wine is not usually served at breakfast, with the delightful exception of sparkling wine which can be served any time, and adds a romantic touch to breakfast, so often a sullen meal.

(Just a suggestion, though; if you're going to mix sparkling wine and orange juice, use an inexpensive wine. There's no point in using French Champagne if you're planning to kill it with fruit juice.)

Veal - A blanc de noir or dry white would probably be a safe bet.

"It's party time, folks."

PARTY TIME

ENTERTAINING WITH WINE

Wine is probably the most versatile drink for entertaining guests. It's probably also the least expensive.

Drinking a fine wine is a unique pleasure, indulging three of our senses: the colour pleases the eye, the taste pleases the palate and the bouquet and aroma please the nose.

An evening of lively chatter and spontaneous laughter is the ideal opportunity for you to share your wines with close friends. With any luck, the sparkle of the wine may rub off on the company.

The problem with trying to serve everybody's favourite drink, however, is that you're sure to disappoint someone. Who was to know that Aunt Milly drank ouzo?

But there's nothing wrong with serving only wines at an evening get-together. In fact, it's rather a smart thing to do, and considered perfectly acceptable in many circles. There are wines that suit each part of the evening, so it's not likely to become boring.

And, after all, it is your party, so you conduct it as you please. Instead of asking: "What will you have to drink?" and then hoping like hell that they won't ask for something impossible, you simply say: "Have a glass of bubbly".

Most people prefer their white wine to be chilled, but do remember that the operative word is 'chilled', not 'frozen'. There is nothing worse than trying to drink wine that has been lying in the fridge for two weeks. Should you wish to chill your wine at all, an hour or two in the fridge should be sufficient.

WHEN GUESTS COME KNOCKING

When the guests arrive, offer them a glass of dry sparkling wine. Aperitifs are served in small, short-stemmed glasses before a meal, and should be neither sweet nor strong. A Méthode Champenoise bubbly would be ideal, but any dry bubbly will do. It cleanses the palate and acts as a good, cheerful ice-breaker without ruining the taste-buds for anything that may come afterwards.

Connoisseurs prefer to serve light wines first, the chilled wines before the warm ones, and the dry whites before the reds. Although there is a lot of merit in the reasoning, the order in which wines are served depends entirely on the individual and the preference of the guests. It's all up to you.

Remember, that if you have added wine to any of your dishes while cooking, it is best to serve the same wine with the dish. If, however, you have chosen to leave the wine for the table, there is a vast range from which you can select for your guests' enjoyment.

When sitting down to a mouth-watering home-cooked meal, treat your guests to a fairly dry sherry with the soup.

Follow this with a fruity, dry white wine with chicken or fish, and a red wine to suit the meat dish - a full-bodied Cabernet for a roast or a hearty stew, or a Shiraz or Pinotage for a mutton dish or a casserole. A Cinsaut-based wine goes really well with Italian dishes.

A sweet fortified Hanepoot or Muscadel will go well with the pudding (or even a noble late harvest, if you can afford it). Fruit steeped in red, white or any fortified wine and served with cream or ice-cream also makes a mouth-watering dessert.

And round off the evening with a selection of cheeses and a glass of fruity port.

There. A whole range of fine wines, each one selected with care to match the dish or the time.

Try THAT with your whisky collection!

UNDER SUNNY SKIES

Braais without wine, is like rugby without Naas, 'pap' without sauce - dry and boring. The 'potjiekos' bubbling in the coals and the smoky aroma of steaks cooking over an open fire, is what the great outdoors is all about. The cave man did it out of necessity, but we do it simply for the exhilaration of being in the sun and the fresh air. And, naturally, the wine!

Even before the convenience of boxed wine and paper cups, South Africans have appreciated the joys of relaxing the way nature intended - crackling fire, sizzling steaks, and a bottle of Tassies.

Wine is ideal for entertaining outdoors. If the 'potjiekos' is drying out, simply add a little heated wine. If the meat needs that extra flavour, sprinkle a little wine and watch the sparks fly. Of course, all that wouldn't be necessary if you had simply marinated the meat in wine in the first place. Remember water adds no flavour to meat, while meat cooked slowly in wine has a unique richness, and because wine is an acid, it also has a tenderising effect.

Braais provide the ideal opportunity for a delicious fruit punch. Add excitement to your braai by letting your imagination run wild and serve your own special blend. Lots of ice, fruit peels and either a white or red wine make a wonderfully refreshing drink. Do remember, however, to add the sparkling wine or Champagne just before serving, otherwise the punch will lose its sparkle. And so will your guests.

THE MORNING AFTER

With all the excitement and festivity of a friendly get-together, there are bound to be a few accidents. Children and unruly adults are the curse of anyone who has happily thrown a party, only to discover that there are half-eaten hors d'oeuvres behind the television, cigarette butts in the geraniums, and red wine all over the carpets.

If you should see Cousin Elliott so engrossed in an animated conversation with a pretty blonde aerobics instructor, that he doesn't realise he is casually tipping red wine on the new carpet, leap into action. Wine stains should be dealt with as soon as possible, because the longer they are left to be absorbed into your carpet (or your clothes), the more difficult they're going to be to remove.

To absorb the wine and stop the stain from spreading, pour salt over the stain. Wait until the salt has absorbed all the wine (you might have to repeat the process a few times), before brushing it up. It might also be a good idea to rub gently with a some soapy water and a little borax just to be sure. Remember, however, to rub in a circular motion to prevent a ring from forming, and to brush the carpet out while it is still damp so that the fibres don't stick together.

If this fails, call in professional carpet-cleaners and forward the bill to Cousin Elliott!

In the pursuit of excellence.

THE PROCESS PERFECTED

THE WINEMAKING PROCESS

Grapes contain all the ingredients necessary for the making of wine.

The recipe for making wine is really quite simple. First, you need a grape with natural yeast on its skin and natural sugar in its juice.

Next, you must break the skin to bring the components together. Then you need a moderately warm temperature (between about five degrees and 31 degrees celsius), as this is the temperature at which the fermentation process works most effectively.

Modern winemakers have discovered, though, that the natural winemaking process is an unpredictable one and can result in some unpleasant surprises.

The bloom on the grape skin contains not only wild yeasts, but also traces of acetobacters, which react with the alcohol to form acetic acid, better known as vinegar.

Some wild yeasts do not perform very well. Some cannot survive in alcohol levels higher than about four percent, for example. So winemakers have discovered that it is more convenient to destroy the wild yeasts and acetobacters right at the beginning of the process, and use specially bred strains of yeast which have a known record of performance. This way the quality of the wine depends less on chance and intuition, but more on skill and expertise. The development of better yeasts has, in fact, become a specialised science.

CRUSHING

In the old days the grapes were crushed by placing them in an open vat and having men or women tread on them with bare feet.

This is, in fact, an ideal method of crushing grapes. Feet are soft and do not crush the pips, which contain bitter oils, or the stalks, which contain harsh tannins, and which may taint the wine.

Some modern presses use inflatable rubber bags to do the job human feet once did so efficiently.

When the grapes arrive at the cellar they are crushed and the stalks removed. The juice is then extracted by pressing.

Pressing techniques vary slightly for red and white grapes. One pressing technique used for both types of grapes simply involves piling the grapes on top of each other and allowing their weight to break the skins. This produces what is known as 'free run juice', which is considered the highest quality available.

The remaining pulp may then be pressed to squeeze out the excess juice, which is called 'press juice'. The pressed grape juice, now ready for fermentation, is called the 'must'.

The juice is pumped into vats which may be sealed. These vats may be made of wood, concrete, fibreglass or stainless steel. Almost all wine producers in the Cape use stainless steel vats.

The skins and stalks left after pressing are used as compost and returned to the vineyards as fertiliser.

FERMENTATION

Fermentation occurs when yeast converts the natural sugar of the grape into alcohol and carbon dioxide. In the process a certain amount of heat is generated.

$$\textbf{YEAST + SUGAR = ALCOHOL + CO}_2 \textbf{ (+ Heat)}$$

(It is important to remember that it is a simplified formula, and that there are many other processes taking place at the same time.)

If we take a look at a single grape berry we'll see that the skin is covered with a dull 'bloom'. This waxy coating contains the spores of natural yeasts, which are usually present in the air.

The pulp of the grape is rich in sugar. The only reason the fermentation process doesn't start while the grape is still on the vine is that the skin separates the sugar from the yeast.

When the skin of the grape is broken, the two main components come into contact and fermentation begins almost at once.

CONTROLLED FERMENTATION

To kill the wild yeast, sulphur dioxide is added to the 'must'. (Better known in South Africa as 'mos' and often used in the making of 'moskonfyt' and 'mosbolletjies' at harvest time.) This has two effects - it absorbs oxygen from the must and forms a coating over the top to prevent air getting to the must.

This coating prevents the wild yeasts and acetobacters from reacting, as they are aerobic and therefore require oxygen to survive.

Wine yeasts are anaerobic, and require no oxygen to be able to work. They can now carry on the fermentation process until all the sugar in the must is converted to alcohol, OR until the alcohol level reaches 16%, killing the yeast and stopping the fermentation, OR until the winemaker decides to stop the process.

The fermentation process may take days or weeks, depending on a number of factors, including the temperature generated by the fermentation and the style of wine the winemaker is trying to achieve. If a 'dry' wine is required, the yeast is allowed to convert all the sugar into alcohol. If a sweeter wine is to be made, the fermentation is stopped while there is still some unfermented sugar (known as 'residual sugar') in the wine.

Yeast is very sensitive to temperature and can only work between the five and 31 degree celsius heat range. If the temperature exceeds these limits, fermentation will stop (this is known in the wine industry as 'stuck fermentation').

A major step towards improving the quality of our wines was the introduction of 'cold fermentation'. The process was introduced to South Africa by Mr NC Krone of Twee Jongegezellen in Tulbagh, and triggered off a whole technological revolution in the industry.

In this process the fermentation tanks are kept at a constantly low temperature by running chilled water over the outside of the tanks or through pipes or water jackets built into the tanks. This slows fermentation considerably, but the real benefit is that the very volatile flavour substances do not evaporate at low temperatures, so the resultant wine is more highly flavoured.

GRAPES BY MOONLIGHT

Harvest time varies according to the local custom, the region and the temperature. Because it is so important to keep grapes cool during the winemaking process, however, several wine farmers prefer to harvest at night. They leave the bunches to cool until about 9pm before starting to pick them.

Other wine farmers start picking very early in the morning and stop when the vineyards begin to warm in the midday sun.

RED WINES

Wine grapes range in colour from deep red to white, but all grape juice is clear (white) in colour. So it is perfectly possible to make white wine from red grapes.

The colour of red wine comes from the grape skins, and the depth of colour depends on the length of time the skins are kept in contact with the juice. If the juice is removed from the skins right away, the result is a white wine (or blanc de noir). Rosé wines are created when the skins of the red grapes are left in the pressed juice for only a few hours. Full-bodied red wines result when the wine is allowed to ferment with the skins.

Heavy red wines pick up not only colour from their skin contact, but also tannin, which is a preservative and helps the wine to age over a long time.

Traditionally, red wine is fermented in open tanks, often made of concrete. The grape skins float to the surface, where they form a 'crust' on the fermenting juice. In order to mix the skins with the juice, cellar workers use wooden 'punches' to punch the crust down into the juice from time to time.

The alcohol formed in the fermentation process extracts the colour and tannin from the skins.

In more modern cellars, red wine is fermented in stainless steel 'roto-tanks' - horizontal tanks which revolve slowly, ensuring that the skins remain in contact with the juice.

IT'S A GAS

Throughout the fermentation process, carbon dioxide gas is released from the wine. If the fermentation is taking place in open vats, the gas simply escapes into the air.

When wines are fermented in closed tanks, some provision must be made for the release of the carbon dioxide. Sealed vats usually have a valve at the top of the tank, which bubbles the gas through water, and prevents air from seeping back into the tank, where it might cause oxidation.

The carbon dioxide produced in the winemaking process can also be trapped by sealing the tank. The gas is absorbed into the wine, and is released in the form of bubbles when the pressure is released. This is one of the methods by which sparkling wines are made.

CLEANING UP

After fermentation, the wine is cloudy, as traces of solids from the grapes and dead yeast cells are suspended in the liquid. These must be removed to produce wine that is brilliantly clear.

The most natural way to purify wine is simply to leave it standing and allow the sediment to settle to the bottom of the tank, and then draw off the clear wine from the top.

This is known as 'racking' the wine.

Another method is to introduce a substance such as egg white or bentonite to the tank. Bentonite is a clay that swells as it absorbs liquid. The bentonite or egg white slowly sinks to the bottom of the tank, collecting the suspended particles as it drops, and leaving the wine clear.

This is called 'fining'.

Wine can also be filtered by pumping it through specialised filters. This is a quick and mechanical process, may leave traces of a 'filter paper' flavour in the wine and also remove some of the wine's unique flavour components.

The final process before bottling is stabilisation. Unstabilised wines tend to produce crystals of tartrates as the wine ages. In days gone by, wines were always decanted to separate the clear wine from the sediment of crystals that had formed in the bottle.

Today most wines are 'stabilised' by chilling them to about four degrees celsius for a while. This forces the tartrate crystals to form and settle at the bottom of the tank, leaving the wine clear.

A GIFT OF NATURE

As we can see, wine is the result of a spontaneous process of nature. The grape has all the necessary constituents to create wine without any assistance from mankind. All man has done is 'perfect' the procedure to suit his own taste and please his own palate.

Dom Perignon discovers the
sparkle of Champagne.

VARIETY IS THE SPICE OF WINE

REDS, WHITES AND FORTIFIED WINES

Wines come in an astonishingly wide variety of styles and categories, from noble old reds to fizzy bubblies and sticky sweet jerepigos. Each has its place in the wine spectrum and most of them will bring out the best in a particular kind of food.

To simplify matters, we have decided to discuss wines in three basic categories: Still wines (also known as 'table wines'), Sparkling wines, and Fortified wines.

STILL WINES

We have seen how yeast reacts with the sugar in grapes to produce alcohol and carbon dioxide.

In the making of still, or table wines, the carbon dioxide gas is allowed to escape, so no bubbles are left in the wine. Fermentation can be stopped at any stage, depending on whether the winemaker is making a semi-sweet or a completely dry wine.

When fermentation ends, the winemaker clarifies the wine, removing the dead yeast cells and other particles, while taking care not to remove any of the essential character of the wine. He then pumps the clear wine into either maturation tanks or wooden casks.

Most white wines are matured in stainless steel tanks, while red wines and some of the heavier whites, (Chardonnay and Sauvignon Blanc) are matured in oak barrels to give them an added flavour.

Wood-matured white wines are becoming popular in South Africa, and winemakers are experimenting with new oak barrels from various parts of the world. The barrels are expensive, however, and wood maturation adds considerably to the final cost of the wine.

BLENDING
Blending is one of the most important aspects of the winemaker's skill and is definitely an art, rather than a science.

75

VARIETY IS THE SPICE OF WINE

There are many reasons for blending wines. Some grape cultivars produce certain desirable qualities, and others produce entirely different ones. If these are harmoniously brought together, the winemaker can capture the best of each cultivar and end up with a more complex and exciting product.

Sometimes old wines, which have become a little dull, can be given a freshness by the addition of younger wines, or sharp, rough young wines can be toned down by adding softer old wine.

Most wines sold in South Africa are brand-name wines and buyers expect to find the same wine under the same label each year.

Wines, however, differ from vintage to vintage, so large wholesale wine producers employ skilled blenders to ensure that each year's wine is as close as possible in character to the previous year's blend.

Blending certainly doesn't imply an inferior wine. In fact, some of the worlds most famous wines - the legendary Chateau wines of France - are the product of skilful blending.

In this respect, winemaking may be compared to orchestral music. Each instrument creates a unique sound, but the art of the conductor is to marry these sounds in exactly the right proportion to create a single, complex and harmonious whole.

After blending, the wine is bottled and often left to mature further, growing softer and more complex all the time. Full-bodied red wines can improve in the bottle for 20 years or more.

WHITE TABLE WINES
White table wines are light coloured and contain between nine and 15% alcohol. They may be very dry or sweet to the palate. White wines are made from green or golden grapes, such as Chenin Blanc, Chardonnay or Riesling, which produce a white juice.

RED TABLE WINES
Red table wines are red or purple in colour and contain between 10% and 15% alcohol (but usually about 12% or 13%). The wine is made from purple or blackish grapes and the colour is obtained from the pigmentation in the grape skins, which are left in the fermenting tanks after crushing.

CATEGORIES
Table wines may be broken down into categories, such as generic wines, Varietal (or 'cultivar') wines and brand-name wines.

Generic wines are those made according to a well-established style, such as claret, or Bordeaux blends, or chianti.

Varietal wines are those made from the juice of a single type of grape, such as Chenin Blanc (often called 'steen' in this country), Cabernet Sauvignon, Pinot Noir and Chardonnay. Varietals are also commonly known as cultivars, a word derived from the term 'cultivated variety'. In fact, many of South Africa's finest wines are known by their cultivar names.

Proprietary brand wines are those which are given a trade mark by which they are advertised and sold, such as Tassenberg, Virginia and Lieberstein. The quality of these wines may vary greatly, but the producers usually prefer to keep the composition of each brand the same, year after year, so they gather a loyal following.

With estate wine it is the producer, and not the wine, which becomes known and trusted. The wine may (and almost certainly will) change from vintage to vintage, but loyal buyers trust that wines from their favourite cellar will always be of an acceptably high standard.

SPARKLING WINE

We have seen how the fermentation process produces carbon dioxide, which is allowed to escape into the air in the making of still wines. If this gas is not permitted to escape, it is absorbed into the wine under pressure, to appear as tiny bubbles when the pressure is released. There are three main methods of getting the carbon dioxide into the wine.

TANK METHOD
This is also known as the 'Charmat Method' or 'cuvée close'. Still wine is placed in a closed tank and sugar and yeast are added to allow a second fermentation to take place. This time the tank is sealed and the gas is absorbed by the wine, which is later filtered and bottled under pressure.

IMPREGNATION METHOD
This is the least expensive method of making sparkling wine, and is also known as the 'carbonization method'. Still wine is simply given an injection of carbon dioxide gas in much the same way as the popular 'Soda Stream' machine adds carbon dioxide to cool drinks.

Although it is the cheapest way to make sparkling wines, modern technology does allow some excellent wines to be made in this way.

MÉTHODE CHAMPENOISE

This is the time consuming traditional method used in the Champagne area of France and today the word 'Champagne' is widely, albeit incorrectly, used to describe any sparkling wine.

A small amount of sugar and yeast is added to still wine to start a second fermentation. The wine is then bottled and sealed temporarily (usually with a crown cork, such as those used on beer bottles). As this second fermentation proceeds, the carbon dioxide cannot escape and is absorbed into the wine.

The process, however, creates a sediment of spent yeast cells, which lies at the bottom of the bottle. To remove this, the bottles are skilfully turned every day (a process called *remuage*) until all the sediment rests on the crown cork.

The necks of the bottles are then placed in a freezing mixture until the wine next to the cork is frozen. This is blown out of the bottle by the pressure of the carbon dioxide when the crown cork is removed. The bottle is topped up with clear sparkling wine and the familiar 'Champagne' cork is inserted and wired down tightly.

Sparkling wine made by this method is often matured for several years before it is sold.

SPARKLE DISCOVERED

Tradition has it that sparkling wine was discovered by the blind Benedictine monk, Dom Perignon, in the 17th Century.

The story is that he was sampling some wine which had started its second fermentation quite by chance. When he felt the bubbles on his tongue, he shouted loudly: "Come quickly, for I think I am tasting the stars".

South African sparkling wine specialist Achim von Arnim has a slightly different theory. He claims that the old monk was fiddling with the bottles in the wine cellar, when one of them popped and the cork hit him on the nose.

Achim's story ends with Dom Perignon shouting: "Come quickly, I am seeing stars!"

Whichever version is true, the old monk's name lives on in one of the most sought-after French Champagnes, Dom Perignon.

FORTIFIED WINES

Fortified wines are produced by adding alcohol (usually in the form of brandy) to still wine during or after fermentation. The alcohol content of these wines is usually between 17% and 22%.

SHERRY

Sherry is made by fermenting wine with a special 'flor' yeast, which floats to the top of the wine, forming a frothy crust. It is an ongoing process, and as wine is siphoned off from under the flor crust, fresh wine is added. This is why sherries do not have particular vintages.

Once the wine has fermented it may be flavoured with a sweet wine and then fortified with brandy.

PORT

Port is made from selected red grape varieties, such as Pontac, Shiraz, Souzão and Tinta Barocca. To ensure a high sugar content, the grapes are allowed to become almost over-ripe before picking.

The winemaker allows the wine to ferment to the desired degree of sweetness, and then stops fermentation by adding brandy.

The basic difference between sherry and port is that sherry is fortified after fermentation is complete, while, in port, the fortification is used to stop fermentation.

The brown colour of tawny port means that it has aged longer than ruby port.

JEREPIGO

This is a popular style of wine among many South African drinkers, but it could be argued that jerepigos are not true wines at all, as no fermentation is involved in the making of these sweet wines.

They are known as 'full sweet' wines, because all the original sugar is retained in the grape juice, which is not fermented at all.

The grapes are crushed and pressed, and then about 17% alcohol is added to the sweet juice to prevent any fermentation.

The best known jerepigos are usually made from Hanepoot (Muscat d'Alexandrie) grapes.

MUSCADELS

Muscadels are made in the same way, but the juice used is that of the white or red Muscadel grape, or Muscat de Frontignan.

A fine Shiraz ~ images of
smoke, leather and cigar boxes.

THE FRUIT OF THE VINE

GRAPES - THE CULTIVARS

Many different 'cultivars'. or varieties of grape are used in the making of wine, and each has its own particular characteristics.

From the farmer's point of view, it is useful to have a variety of cultivars, each ripening at a different time, so the harvest is spread out comfortably over a long period, and it is not necessary to rush to pick all the grapes when they ripen at the same time.

Each cultivar has its own preferences for the type of soil or climatic conditions in which it grows best, so cultivars can be selected to make the best use of each part of the farm. In winemaking, the cultivars are sometimes used on their own, and sometimes they are blended with others to form a more complex or interesting wine.

Wine tasters soon get to know what sort of flavours to expect from each cultivar, and can say at a sip whether the wine has a typical 'varietal character'.

These varietal characteristics tend to be most prominent when the wine is young, and fade with age, making way for a more mellow, mature character.

A young Shiraz, for example, will probably taste and smell quite strongly of the typical cigar-boxy, smoke or leather Shiraz character. After several years of maturation that character will fade, an old Shiraz may be mistaken for old Cabernets, even by experienced tasters.

South African wine drinkers set great store by the 'cultivars' of the grapes from which their wine was made. This is probably because the old Wine of Origin system included a special stripe on the neck label for a wine from a particular cultivar, as opposed to a wine blended from several cultivars.

It's not vital to know the cultivar of a wine, particularly if you enjoy brand-name wines like Tassenberg or Honey Blossom.

But for those who like to chat knowledgeably about such things, here is a list of some of the common wine grape cultivars on the Cape winelands, and the kind of flavour tasters expect from each.

WHITES

Bukettraube: Introduced to South Africa only in the 1970s', this vigorous grower produces grapes which ripen early creating a spicy wine, often with a delicate Muscat aroma.

Chardonnay: This grape is the backbone of the famous Burgundy, Chablis and Champagne of France, and is now grown everywhere from Australia to California. Currently, it is the most fashionable of all the wine grapes grown in South Africa. In fact, there is so much of it being planted, and so much Chardonnay being made, that it looks set to flood the market. Producers like it because they can charge exorbitant prices. But just wait until the market is saturated!

Two distinct styles are made. One has a character reminiscent of butterscotch, the other is like citrus or melons. It is one of the few white wine varieties usually made with some wood maturation to add a rich complexity.

Chenel: A cross between Chenin Blanc and Trebbiano, Chenel is grown more in the high production inland areas, than at the coast.

Chenin Blanc (sometimes called **Steen**): This is a wonderfully versatile white grape and is the most widely planted variety in the country, making up about 30% of all wine grapes in the Cape. Good steen makes anything from fine, dry, flinty wines, through all degrees of sweetness, right up to noble late harvests. Chenin Blanc ripens in mid-season, and has a grassy or steely flavour when picked young, but may acquire a guava character if picked later.

Clairette Blanche: This late-maturing grape has a low acidity and it is regularly used in the making of sparkling wines. The grapes ripen late in the harvest.

Colombar (or **Colombard**): Colombar was originally grown for making brandy, until it was used in the Robertson area for wine. Only then did producers realise its potential. Colombars have a distinctive guava nose and there are some excellent easy-drinking wines made from this cultivar, particularly from the Robertson area.

Fernão Pires: This early ripening Portuguese grape is doing quite well in the Cape, and a few good wines are being made from it, so be on the look-out for some real bargains from this cultivar.

Gewürztraminer: This is an important wine grape in the Alsace region of France, but has produced some good wines locally, particularly in the coastal and Tulbagh regions. It ripens early and should produce wines with a spicy character.

Kerner: Another recently-introduced grape, Kerner produces a distinctive, although rather 'stern' wine. Farmers like it because it ripens very easily.

Muscat: There are several varieties of Muscat, probably the best known being Muscat d'Alexandrie, or Hanepoot. It is undoubtedly South Africa's favourite grape and is used in the best jerepigos. The grapes ripen fairly late, and are usually only harvested when they are very ripe to get the maximum sugar. The result is a highly scented, honey-flavoured wine.

Rhine Riesling (also called **Weisser Riesling**): This variety often has a slightly 'paraffin' nose, which is not unpleasant, but easily identified. It is relatively new to the Cape and produces a far more fragrant wine than our old Cape Riesling. Rhine Riesling is very popular in German wines and is certainly more fashionable than Cape Riesling at the moment, but don't scorn our local variety. It still produces some very fine wines.

Riesling (**Cape** or **South African Riesling**): This is not a true Riesling at all, but mistakenly labelled Riesling many years ago, and the name has been retained. It is famous locally for producing very elegant, steely dry white wine, often with a crisp acid bite to it. It's grown mainly in the coastal regions.

Sauvignon Blanc: Wines made from this cultivar vary in style, but are usually rich in flavour, and some exceptional blends using Sauvignon Blanc are created in Bordeaux in France. Although once popular in South Africa, it fell from favour but has now made a reappearance and recent efforts have shown some encouraging wines. Locally, it is becoming increasingly popular and is being planted extensively in all South African wine areas. Many producers experiment with various styles, including wooded and unwooded. If the wine is wood-matured, it is often labelled 'blanc fumé'.

Sémillon (Green Grape): Today there's not much of this around, although it was once popular in the early days of South African winemaking. Sémillon is used in France for creating dry Graves and sweet Sauternes wines. There is some renewed interest in this grape locally, and chances are it could become a cult wine in the not too distant future.

White French: Known locally as White French or Fransdruif, this wine is called Palomino in Spain, where it is used in sherry production. It is rapidly declining in popularity due to its vulnerability to the disease Anthracnose.

REDS

Cabernet Blanc: Related to Cabernet Sauvignon, but usually produces a much softer wine, so they are ideal blending partners. Not much Cabernet Blanc is grown in South Africa, but a few farmers are planting it for blending.

Cabernet Sauvignon: The king of cultivars, this fruity and juicy grape is used in most of the Chateau wines of France. It produces a wine of great ageing potential and a wide range of styles. There's little to beat a well-matured and carefully made Cabernet Sauvignon wine. A real treat.

Cinsaut (formerly called **Hermitage**): Cinsaut is the most widely grown red wine grape in South Africa and, although it is not particularly fashionable, it is used in most of the bulk-produced budget red wines, such as Tassenberg.

Gamay Noir: This grape is used in the young Beaujolais-Nouveau wines made for very early drinking, and will probably become increasingly popular as the Nouveau trend catches on. It can, however, make excellent ageing wines.

Merlot: This is becoming an increasingly popular wine. It is usually grown for blending with Cabernet Sauvignon, but Cape winemakers are discovering that it makes an exceptionally good wine on its own under local conditions. It is one of the main components of Bordeaux-style blends.

Pinot Noir: This is the great red cultivar of Burgundy, and is grown only in small quantities in South Africa. There are, however, some fine wines made from the cultivar locally. Pinot Noir has an almost blackberry flavour.

Pinotage: This is South Africa's first successful crossing, developed from Pinot Noir and Hermitage. It makes wine with a distinctive 'duco' nose, particularly when young. This acetone character disappears with age, however, and they can mature into a really great, soft wine. Pinotage seems to be most successful in the coastal areas.

Shiraz: Grown mostly in the coastal area, and to a smaller extent in the Breede River area, Shiraz produces well-flavoured wines, reminiscent of old leather saddlery or cigar boxes. Shiraz wines have a small, but very loyal following.

TIME WILL TELL

MATURATION - FACT OR FABLE?

Much is written and spoken about the maturing, or ageing, of wine. Buyers often ask whether a particular wine should be drunk immediately or 'laid down' to mature for a few years. While most white wines do not need to be bottled for long and should, in fact, be drunk within one or two years, it is generally accepted that red wines improve with age.

Let's not forget, however, that wine is in fact an intermediate product. If it is allowed to run its natural course it will change from fresh new wine into smooth old wine, then into flat, characterless old wine and finally into vinegar.

So it is changing all the time.

But there are certain natural components of wine which act as preservatives and slow down these changes. The best known of these are alcohol, tannin and residual sugar.

If a wine is high in these components, it will certainly last a long time and probably improve over a number of years. Tannins change with time, from being the astringent, mouth-puckering harsh tannins often found in young red wines, to the so-called 'soft tannins' which are smooth and inoffensive, characteristics associated with well-matured red wines.

In fortified wines, such as port and sherry, the alcohol, which was added artificially, and not produced by natural fermentation, is usually rough and may burn the throat at first. As time passes, however, this added alcohol 'marries' with the grape juice and becomes smoother and more mellow.

One of the important factors which influences a wine's maturation is the amount of air in contact with the wine's surface.

Since the size of a bottle neck is more or less constant, the amount of air in contact with the wine in a small bottle is proportionately larger than that in a larger bottle, so the contents of a half bottle of wine will mature faster that a magnum.

True perfection is only a
matter of time.

This is one of the reasons why a magnum will usually fetch a higher price than two smaller bottles of the same wine. The smaller surface area allows the wine in the magnum to mature slower, and therefore to last longer.

And, as with most winemaking processes, wine that has matured slowly is invariably better than wine which has matured quickly.

COLOUR

Time also has a marked effect on the colour of a wine. A young white wine will usually start off as an almost clear liquid, with a possible green tinge.

As the wine ages, it will develop a straw colour, and later a deep golden hue, and eventually a shade of amber.

Young red wines begin life purple or violet and grow steadily toward a brick colour, and eventually brown.

VINTAGES

Vintage charts are often drawn up in an attempt to show which years produced the best wines, but these are apt to be generalisations and could result in buyers missing out on some excellent wines.

The greatest limitation of any vintage chart is that it must of necessity make generalisations about the various regions.

But each region contains a number of micro-climates, depending on the height above sea level of a particular farm, the local winds, the shading of the soil and many other factors, which may affect the vine and quality of wine. Wines produced from a particular vineyard may, therefore, differ quite considerably from those produced on a neighbouring farm.

Another danger of vintage charts is that they cannot take into account the way the wine has been stored since it was made.

Badly handled and stored wine can be a disappointment, no matter how good it was when it was originally made.

Labour of love.

FROM THE SOIL TO THE CELLAR

AN AGRICULTURAL PRODUCT

We should never forget that wine is an agricultural product, no less than butter or cheese. And our enjoyment of wine is enhanced if we know a little about its agricultural background.

We might then realise why wine is sometimes rather an expensive commodity. It's certainly not just another fruit simply plucked from vines free of charge and crammed into bottles.

Farmers, for some strange reason, are often regarded with some scorn by townsfolk. "All you farm folk do is sit around all year, waiting for the fruit to ripen, and then make some wine in summer", seems to be the usual attitude. Farmers wake up in the morning, feed the chickens, milk the cow and turn on the sprinklers. Then they spend the afternoon counting their money, until it's time for sun-downers on the *stoep* and watch the sun set over their land. City folk have to work all year round, but farmers have one long holiday. Right? Wrong.

In fact, every season is a busy one for the wine farmer. It costs thousands of rands to establish a single hectare of vineyard. The ground must be cleared of bushes and rocks, an operation usually involving costly earth-moving machinery. Then the soil must be analyzed and prepared by deep ploughing or 'subsoiling', and chemical fertilisers must be added to correct any imbalances.

Modern wine farmers take great care to test the soil on every portion of their land, and to plant the grape variety that will fare best in that type of soil and that particular micro-climate. The vine stocks must then be bought and planted, and trellises erected to support the vines as they grow.

Wine farming has meant heavy machinery, expensive plant material, expensive chemicals and plenty of rather expensive farm labour. Wages have to be paid whether there is income or not.

All this must be paid immediately, of course, but the farmer then has to wait about five years before there is any return on his money.

TENDING THE LAND

Meanwhile, the established vines on the farm are keeping everybody on the hop.

In spring the nodes on the vine shoots start to swell, and in late October the vines flower and are pollinated. This is one of the vital stages that determines the size of the crop later.

The soil around each vine must be loosened, and often a dressing of fertiliser is applied. Weeds must be eliminated. Spring showers may bring fungus diseases, and these must be eliminated by spraying.

Summer is the time for ripening, and in some areas the soil must be irrigated. Growth of the vines is carefully monitored, and vines that show too much growth are topped to prevent sagging and wind damage. For high quality wines, a low yield of grapes per hectare is sometimes required, so excess bunches are picked.

Cellar machinery is checked and serviced in preparation for the pressing season.

The grape harvest begins late in summer, and this is the busiest time of the year. The grapes are carefully watched until they reach optimum ripeness. They are then picked, brought to the cellar, crushed, destalked and fermented. For a few short weeks all the expensive crushing, destalking and bottling machinery that has stood idle for most of the year, is brought into full operation.

In autumn, when the harvest is finally over, the vineyards must be prepared for winter. The first pruning, known as 'stripping', is carried out and the vines are sometimes given a dusting of sulphur to prevent fungus diseases from developing during winter.

In winter the vines are pruned and the entire cycle starts again.

And, to top it all, there's the added concern of trying to sell the year's wine production, handling visitors to the cellar and deciding exactly what type of wine to make from each grape harvest.

SETTING A TREND

Although wine is an agricultural product, it differs from all other produce in one important aspect - it is subject to the whims and foibles of fashion.

People buy butter, eggs, wheat and meat constantly from year to year, but when it comes to wine, fashions change regularly and often suddenly. One year the trend might be towards heavy red wines. The next season reds might be passé and the socially 'elite' may be drinking blancs de noir or dry white wines.

There's no logical reason for it. Trendsetters moving in all the 'right' social circles, might decide that pink wines are 'in', so everybody flushes their white wines down the loo and dashes off to the nearest bottle store to stock up on pinks.

The problem is that it takes at least five years for a vineyard to achieve production, so it's no use at all trying to follow fashion.

If your fields are about to yield an impressive crop of Cabernet Sauvignon, and the leaders of fashion suddenly decree that Chardonnay is THE drink, that's just tough luck.

No matter how big the harvest, or how much wine you've managed to bottle, it counts for nothing unless there are people out there willing to buy it.

An easy life? Maybe it's simpler just to be a heart surgeon. On the other hand, it's probably easier for a failed wine farmer to drown his financial sorrows.

ON SHOW!

In their advertising, wine producers often mention the awards their products have won on shows throughout the world. This can be confusing to wine drinkers.

What is a 'champion' wine? How important is it for a winemaker to be 'Winemaker of the Year' or 'Regional Champion'?

In South Africa the primary competition for winemakers is the series of regional young wine shows that takes place about six months after the pressing season every year. These culminate in the South African Championship Wine Show held at the Cape Show grounds in Goodwood in November.

At this show the annual National Champion Winemaker is judged on the overall points scored in every category and there are sections for Champion Private Producer, Estate Winemaker and Co-operative Winemaker.

The status of 'champion' is also awarded for various categories of wine, such as Dry White Table Wine, Red Table Wine, Fortified Wine and Natural Sweet Table Wine.

These young wine shows are, as the name implies, for young wines still in tanks, vats or casks, so they are of more interest to wine producers than to wine consumers. It is rare that a winning wine will appear in the bottle stores in that form. Most are eventually blended with other wines, or marketed under brand-names.

Still, one must accept in principle that a cellar that is a consistent winner is likely to be better than one which does not win awards.

Regional young wine shows take place in Stellenbosch, Paarl, Worcester, Robertson and the Olifants River areas. But, remember that major brands, such as Fleur du Cap, Nederburg, Zonnebloem and others do not compete in these young wine shows.

IN THE BOTTLE

Of far more interest to wine drinkers are the bottled wine shows where the products on show are available to the consumer through the general trade.

Only two regions hold regular bottled wine shows, and these are the Stellenbosch and Robertson regions. It is well worth attending these events to taste the wines and make notes for future buying.

STATUS

One wine competition that carries considerable status is the annual Diners Club Winemaker of the Year Award.

Each year a particular category of wine is stipulated, and wine-makers submit wines of that category for judging. Past categories have included Cabernet Sauvignon of the 1980 vintage, Rhine Rieslings of the '82 and '83 vintages, Sauvignon Blancs from 1984, Gewürztraminers from '84 and '85, fortified Muscat Dessert Wines and Chardonnays.

The winner is given an overseas trip to any winemaking country of his or her choice.

FOREIGN SHORES

South African wines are also exhibited at a number of shows overseas, where they often fare extremely well against competition from other countries.

The two most prestigious of these exhibitions are the Monde Selection and the annual International Wine and Spirit Competition staged by the British Club Oenologique, where the prize-giving is usually held in the British House of Commons' dining room.

UNDER THE HAMMER

Wine auctions are becoming a regular feature of our wine scene. The best known of these is probably the Nederburg Auction, which has been running annually since 1975.

There is also the annual Independent Winemakers' Guild Auction, and more recently the New World Wine Auction.

Wine auctions and competitions add to the public's appreciation of the value of fine and rare wines. They may not, however, be of direct interest to the ordinary drinker who simply likes a glass of chilled plonk with his evening braai.

Would you be able to relax with a wine if you know it's costing you R100 a sip?

Wine auctions have also become a popular way of raising money for charity, but these are of very little benefit to either the wine industry or the consumer, other than the satisfaction that they are helping the needy.

"Aah, now THAT'S a fine wine".

THE CAPE VINTAGE GUIDE

21 YEARS OF FINE WINES

As we have seen, the South African wine industry has a proud history dating back to the days of van Riebeeck. The following is an assessment of the wines produced in the last 21 years.

The quality of wines naturally vary from year to year, and your enjoyment of those wines may depend on when you drink them. Do not, however, apply this guide rigidly as even in a poor year individual cellars may produce some excellent wines.

1970 This was a hot but wet vintage. Early rains affected the early ripening Pinotage. Conditions were ideal for later-ripening red varieties such as Shiraz and Cabernet Sauvignon.

1971 A large crop and at the time generally considered to be of average quality. Some of the reds developed well with time, but most have long passed their best.

1972 A hot, dry vintage and acclaimed as being one of our greats - exceptional for reds, particularly Cabernet Sauvignon.

1973 A small crop in which downy mildew gave problems and rain affected the late-ripening reds. It is generally considered that the whites of this vintage were better than the reds, and although some Cabernets developed well, most should have been drunk by now.

1974 A very dry year. The consistent warmth produced high sugars and is considered by many as the outstanding vintage of the decade for reds. In general the whites suffered, although some Steens proved exceptional. The overall crop was down in quantity owing to poor setting conditions in the spring. Generally, the 1974 Cabernets are still showing well, although many have now reached their best.

1975 A fairly dry vintage with a hot February which resulted in whites of very low acid; late rains tended to spoil the late-ripening reds, especially Cabernet, although there are some exceptions.

1976 A long, cold winter with late rains and snow. The vintage took place in almost ideal conditions and all cultivars produced good quantity and quality. The reds are proving to be outstanding.

1977 A cool winter followed by a wet spring and poor berry set. The harvest was troubled with rain and was plagued by extensive downy mildew. The Cape Riesling crop was small but produced some excellent wines. High acids benefited all whites and gave reds a very French character, although they generally lacked colour. Red varietals showed well, but most have peaked by now.

1978 Another cool wet winter followed by rains which kept sugars low. Considered to be a vintage of good quality and quantity.

1979 The driest and warmest winter since 1926. February was warm and wet and resulted in a high incidence of botrytis which in some areas developed into noble rot. March was dry and cool so late-ripening reds showed rather well, but most are not great.

1980 Overall a good vintage with some exciting wines. Hot dry weather gave sound grapes with good sugars, but low acids. Cabernets and Cabernet-based blends are beginning to show very well.

1981 The year of the great flood at Laingsburg. This deluge did untold damage to many winemaking areas in the Robertson, Montagu and Bonnievale areas. The cool weather from flowering to pressing resulted in relatively higher fruit acids in all wines. Quality within wine types varied and some exceptionally good white wines were produced. Red grapes tended to lack sugar and colour and the wines they produced proved lighter than usual.

1982 The biggest crop to that date with the high quality areas of Stellenbosch, Paarl, Durbanville and Constantia increasing by 20%. Almost perfect climatic conditions, however, enabled superb wines to be made. Some better reds now released show excellent character.

1983 The crop was up 5% on the record harvest of 1982 and it was a sound vintage, although acid and sugar levels were generally lower than in 1982. Some great wines were made, but overall 1983 did not match the great vintage of '82. Some cooler areas were exceptions and the wines, as well as normal crop loads, are well-balanced and developing better than expected.

1984 The 1984 vintage was disease-free but slightly down on 1983. It was preceded by one of the wettest winters in ten years. Late bud burst meant that the harvest began some ten days later than in 1983.

A long, dry period from October to February caused some white varieties (such as Cape Riesling, Colombar and Steen, growing on shallow, sandy soils in the Coastal Region) to ripen under stress. This gave high sugars but low acid which led to rather neutral wines. The reds, however, were magnificent, Cabernet being helped by some late rains. The late red cultivars produced excellent colour and a variety of red wine styles which are ageing well.

1985 A greater range of style and variety of wine was produced from the 1985 vintage than ever before. The total crop was almost 10% down on 1984 and, with a few notable exceptions, whites were generally better than reds. Cool conditions and frequent rains during the ripening period produced grapes with good acid/sugar ratio. The 1985 season was probably one of the longest on record. The whites are exceptionally fragrant with an ideal sugar/acid balance. Red wines have good flavour but are lighter than those of 1984.

1986 The hottest, driest summer for a long time. In most areas the vintage started four weeks earlier than usual. Crops were down in quantity, the late-ripening Cabernet Sauvignon being most affected. Winemakers were delighted with the quality of grapes and expected some excellent wines as the fruit acids were good despite the heat.

1987 The overall yield was down by approximately 10% on the 1986 vintage, due mainly to rot attacking the grapes, but the long, cool growing season ensured optimum ripeness in healthy grapes.

The outstanding characteristic of the vintage, particularly of wines from the Coastal Region, was the balanced combination of high fixed acidity, low pH and good sugar. This resulted in fruity white and red wines with good cellaring potential.

1988 The very long, cool ripening season ended very abruptly mid-vintage with four weeks of excessive heat, which brought a good deal of the crop to ripeness at much the same time. In general the cooler areas seem to have potentially good wines from the better cultivars, such as Cabernet Sauvignon, Cape Riesling, Steen and Pinotage. Some magnificent sweet dessert wines have been made.

1989 A good winter chilling occurred and the vines experienced normal and natural bud burst, unlike the previous two vintages. It was a dry year with no late rains, although a cool spring lasting until the end of December, resulted in slightly later ripening conditions. All these factors resulted in improved quality and a greater concentration of flavour components. A late heat-wave adversely affected some Cabernets and Rieslings. This was the first 'real' Chardonnay vintage: the vines enjoyed the drought conditions and the fruit ripened superbly, and good quantities were made by many producers. This vintage was the healthiest in many years; virtually no spraying for disease was required. A sound vintage with some excellent wines, especially Cabernets and Chardonnays.

1990 This was not an easy vintage as much of the top quality crop ripened at the same time, instead of being well spaced. It seems, however, that most winemakers are happy with what they have in their cellars and appear to be delighted with their Cabernet, Merlot, Chardonnay and Sauvignon Blanc.

With the earlier ripening clones now well established, the vintage seems to begin earlier and earlier. In the Robertson area where the vintage traditionally began in mid-February, they were in full swing by the end of January. In this area, as well as the Breede River region, it appears to have been a 'normal' harvest judging by crop size. The quality is generally better than expected.

Sauvignon Blanc has better character than last year and reports have been received of some very good Colombars and excellent Steens. Cape Riesling also seems to have had a good year, while aromatic vines, like Gewürztraminer, are showing well. The Robertson area is traditionally a fortified wine producer and this year the Muscadels and Hanepoots are exceptionally good.

All reports from the Coastal Region indicate a bumper crop with generally good quality and an excellent Cabernet. The relatively cool ripening period ended abruptly with a very hot spell from mid to late February. Sugars suddenly developed and a lot of Steen and Pinotage ripened rapidly. This spell was, however, followed by about five centimetres of rain that caused rot in the Steen. Fortunately, the Cape Doctor (south-easterly wind) blew strongly after the rain and dried the vineyards well. The early Chardonnay seems to be good in areas ranging from Constantia, through Durbanville and Stellenbosch, to Paarl and the largest amount ever was harvested this year as the new plantings were ready. This vintage's Sauvignon Blanc is of far greater quality than last year's, while the old stalwarts, Cape Riesling and early Steen, seem to have been good even though the latter was reduced in volume by the rot that followed the rain. A lot of noble late harvests have been made, especially in the Stellenbosch and Durbanville areas, possibly far more than the market can accommodate.

The pride of this year's vintage, however, seems to be Cabernet Sauvignon. All cellars are producing excellent colours, good sugar/acid ratios and fine flavours. This, backed by the best Merlot ever, makes the first vintage of the 1990s potentially very exciting.

HITTING THE WINE TRAIL

THE WINE ROUTES OF THE CAPE

The subject of wine and wine tasting becomes far more exciting and personal if you are lucky enough to visit a wine cellar and watch the winemaking process.

It also adds to your enjoyment if you've met the winemaker and chatted about some of the wines.

We are fortunate to have several well-organised wine routes in the Cape, where wine lovers can see at first hand where the vines are grown, how their favourite wines are made, and often meet the people who made them.

The Stellenbosch Wine Route - the first wine route to be established in the Cape - has become one of the most popular tourist attractions in the region, second only to Table Mountain in the number of tourists it attracts annually.

Like any outing, a visit to a wine estate will be more informative and more enjoyable if you do a little homework before you set out.

Every wine route publishes a detailed map of the cellars on the route. Study the guide and decide which estates you'd like to visit. If you're planning your visit for a Saturday, check which ones are open during the afternoon, so you don't arrive to find the place closed.

Most wine routes have erected clear signposts showing the member cellars and carrying the distinctive emblem of the particular wine route, so it's easy to find your way around.

As a general rule, wine estates produce more individually-styled wines. Each wine is produced under the careful supervision of the owner or manager, who starts off, right from the vine planting stage, with a definite kind of wine in mind. Quantities are often very limited. For these reasons, estate wines tend to be a little more expensive than co-op wines. Wine co-operatives usually sell the bulk of their products to the big wine wholesalers. The wines that are bottled under the co-op's own labels are sold mainly to keep the name of the particular co-op in the public eye.

Eureka!

Co-op wines are often very reasonably priced and there are some excellent bargains to be found there.

On your first visit to a wine route try to call in at one estate and one co-op during the morning, planning your route to include at least one cellar tour.

Several wine producers on the wine routes offer light meals in peaceful country settings. It might be a good idea to plan a lunchtime visit to one of these cellars and combine lunch with a tasting.

Some cellars are happy to allow visitors to taste their wines free of charge, while others charge a nominal fee for a tasting. The cellar managers who charge for tastings say they do it to prevent freeloaders from using the wine route simply as a free booze supply. Fair enough.

Wine tasting and buying should not be a hurried affair. Give yourself time to sample several wines at each cellar you visit, but have at least some idea of the sort of wines you're likely to enjoy, so you don't waste time sipping tannic young red wines if what you really enjoy are semi-sweet white ones.

On the other hand, a wine tasting is an occasion to encounter new wines, so be a little adventurous.

If, after visiting two cellars in the morning and a third for lunch, you still feel like tasting wines, make sure that at least one member of the party abstains to ensure a safe drive home.

If you want to be very safe, try an organised coach tour of the Wine Route, then the driving is somebody else's problem.

THE FAIREST CAPE

The best known wine routes of the Cape are:

• **The Stellenbosch Wine Route**, which offers a very wide variety of wines, from elegant dry whites to wood-matured reds and ports. There are several co-operative wineries for bargain hunters, and a number of famous wine estates.

Most of the big wine wholesalers have cellars in Stellenbosch. The wine route offers a variety of other attractions, from museums and art galleries to restaurants.

• **The Paarl Wine Route** may be relatively small, but includes some estates and cellars well worth visiting. The KWV headquarters are in Paarl, and the famous Nederburg winery is nearby, and has recently been given a licence to sell wine from the farm. The area produces many fine wines in a variety of styles.

• **The Vignerons of Franschhoek** concentrate on very elegant, stylish wines in the French tradition. Wines from this cool valley are often expensive and not many of the farms are open to visitors, except by appointment.

Sparkling wines from Franschhoek are almost invariably made in the traditional Méthode Champenoise. One farm, Clos Cabrière, produces only sparkling wines. Boschendal is probably the best known estate in the picturesque valley, and there are several excellent restaurants in the town.

• **The Robertson Wine Trust**, originally known for its sweet fortified wines, now produces some very elegant table wines. A speciality of the Robertson region is its Colombard wine. Most of the cellars open to the public are co-operatives, and there are some good bargains to be found.

• **The Worcester Wine Route** consists mostly of co-operatives, and the accent is on value for money. The town has some fine restaurants and an interesting agricultural museum.

• **The West Coast Wine Route**. Wine seems to be of secondary interest here. The friendly and fun-loving people of the west coast offer an amazing array of seafood specialities, a spectacular season of wild flower displays, wilderness areas for hiking, and traditional products from bokkoms to boots. Vredendal boasts the largest co-operative winery in the country.

• **The Constantia Wine Route** is where it all started. Constantia is the Cape's oldest wine area. There are three wine-producing farms on the Constantia Wine Route.

All three of these historical estates - Groot Constantia, Klein Constantia and Buitenverwachting, are within 15 minutes' drive from the city centre and all three offer tastings and cellar tours.

Groot Constantia has the unusual distinction of being the only wine cellar in South Africa that is legally entitled to stay open for wine tours and sales on Sundays.

ADDRESSES
The following addresses and telephone numbers may be useful
should you want to visit some of the cellars and wine farms on the
Cape's famous wine routes.

Stellenbosch Wine Route -   P O Box 204
Stellenbosch
7600
Tel: (02231) 4310

Paarl Wine Route -   P O Box 46
Paarl
7620
Tel: (02211) 23605

Robertson Wine Trust -   P O Box 550
Robertson
6705
Tel: (02351) 3167

Constantia Wine Route -   Private Bag Constantia
7848
Tel: (021) 794 5179
or (021) 794 5128

Captour -   P O Box 1403
Cape Town
8000
Tel: (021) 462 2040

SA Tourism Board -   Satour
Private Bag X9108
Cape Town
8000 ⁕
Tel: (021) 21 6274

Springbok Atlas Safaris -   P O Box 115
Cape Town
8000
Tel: (021) 419 2244

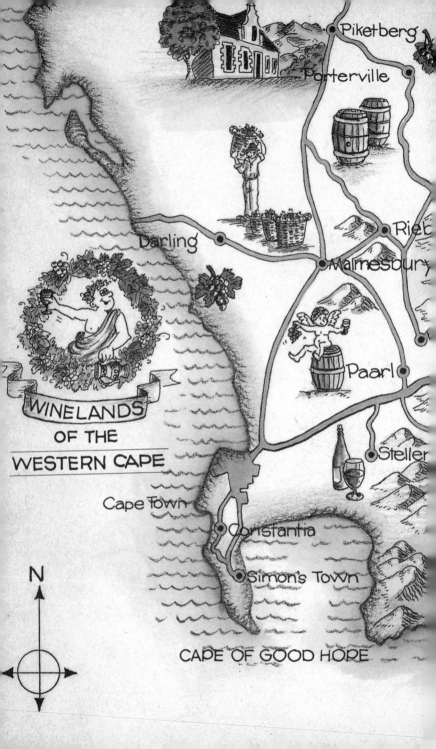

Happiness is...

OUT AND ABOUT

WINE PRODUCERS

The wines and the winelands of South Africa are world famous. Some of the world's most distinguished connoisseurs travel to our shores simply to sample our wines and enjoy the pastoral beauty of the Cape. But these rare pleasures are not reserved for the international winemaking community, or even for the tourist. Because some of the world's finest wines are made on your own doorstep, the pleasure should be yours, too.

The following is a list of wine producers who have either opened their estates to the public or may be willing to arrange a private tour. Not all of the estates and co-operatives listed are licensed to trade, but visit them anyway. It's a wonderful opportunity to learn about wines, the winemaking process, to sample some exquisite wines and, at the same time, savour the splendour of the majestic Cape.

Aan-de-Doorns Co-op P O Box 235, Worcester 6850; Tel: (0231) 72301. Winemaker: Alwyn Mostert. Weekdays 07h30 - 12h00; 13h00 - 17h30; Saturdays 09h00 - 12h00.

Agterkliphoogte Co-op P O Box 267, Robertson 6705; Tel: (02351) 2155. Winemaker: Helmard Hanekom. Weekdays 08h00 - 12h00, 13h30 - 17h00.

Allesverloren Estate P O Box 23, Riebeek-Wes 6800; Tel: (02246) 320. Winemaker: Fanie Malan. Visitors by appointment only.

Alphen (*see* **Stellenzicht**)

Alto Estate P O Box 184, Stellenbosch 7600; Tel: (02231) 93884. Winemaker: Hempies du Toit. Visitors by appointment only.

Altydgedacht Estate P O Box 213, Durbanville 7550; Tel: (021) 961295. Winemaker: Oliver Parker; Vineyards: John Parker. Wednesdays 14h00 - 18h00 and Saturdays 09h00 - 12h00.

Ashton Co-op P O Box 40, Ashton 6715; Tel: (0234) 51135. Winemaker: Tertius Siebrits. Weekdays 08h00 - 12h30; 13h30 - 17h30. Christmas and Easter periods open Saturdays 08h00 - 13h00.

Aufwaerts Co-op P O Box 51, Rawsonville 6845; Tel: (0231) 91196. Winemaker: C de Villiers. Visitors by appointment only.

Avontuur P O Box 1128, Somerset West 7130; Tel: (024) 553450. Winemaker: Manie Kloppers. Weekdays 09h00 - 17h30; Saturdays 09h00 - 13h00.

Backsberg Estate P O Box 1, Klapmuts 7625; Tel: (02211) 5141. Winemaker: Wynand Hamman; Weekdays 08h00 - 17h30; Saturdays and public holidays 08h00 - 13h00.

Badsberg Co-op Grootvlakte, P O Box 72, Rawsonville 6845; Tel: (0231) 91120. Winemaker: Gerrit van Zyl. Mondays to Fridays 08h00 - 17h00; Saturdays 09h00 - 12h00.

Barrydale Co-op P O Box 59, Barrydale 6750; Tel: (02971) 12. Winemaker: Bob de Villiers. Mondays to Thursdays 08h30 - 17h30; Fridays 08h30 - 17h00; Saturdays 08h30 - 13h00.

Bellingham Wines Union Wines Limited, P O Box 246, Wellington 7655; Tel: (02211) 31001. Winemaker: Johan Schreuder. December to April four tastings per day at 09h30, 10h30, 14h30, 15h30 and Saturdays at 10h30. Closed to public during the rest of the season.

Bergkelder Private Bag X5001, Stellenbosch 7600; Tel: (02231) 73480. Cellar master: Dr Julius Laszlo. Regular cellar tours offered at 10h00 and 15h00, or by special arrangement.

Bergsig Estate P O Box 15, Breë-rivier 6858; Tel: (02324) 603. Winemaker: Kas Huisamen. Weekdays 08h30 - 12h00, 13h30 - 17h00 and Saturdays 09h00 - 12h00.

Blaauwklippen P O Box 54, Stellenbosch 7600; Tel: (02231) 900133/4. Winemaker: Jacques Kruger. Weekdays 08h30 - 12h00, 14h00 - 17h00 and Saturdays 08h30 - 12h30.

Bloemendal Estate P O Box 466, Durbanville 7550; Tel: (021) 962682. Winemaker: Jackie Coetzee. Wednesdays 13h00 - 18h00 and Saturdays 09h00 - 12h00.

Bolandse Co-op P O Box 2, Huguenot 7645; Tel: (02211) 626190/1 (Daljosophat Branch) and P O Box 7007, Paarl, 7645; Tel: (02211) 21766/21747/8 (Northern Paarl Branch). Winemakers: A Roussouw and A B le Roux; Weekdays 08h30 - 12h30, 13h30 - 17h30 and Saturdays 09h00 - 12h00.

Bon Courage Estate P O Box 589, Robertson 6705; Tel: (02351) 4170/8 or 4557. Winemaker: Andre Bruwer. Weekdays 09h00 - 12h00, 14h00 - 17h00.

Bonnievale Co-op P O Box 206, Bonnievale 6730; Tel: (02346) 2795. Winemaker: Piet Linde. Weekdays 08h30 - 12h30, 13h30 - 17h00.

Boplaas Estate P O Box 156, Calitzdorp 6660; Tel: (04437) 326. Winemaker: Carel Nel. Weekdays 08h00 - 13h00, 14h00 - 17h00; Saturdays 09h00 - 12h30.

Boschendal Estate Groot Drakenstein 7680; Tel: (0211) 41031. Winemaker: Hilko Hegewisch; Vineyards: Herman Hanekom. Weekdays 08h30 - 13h00, 14h00 - 17h00 and Saturdays 08h30 - 12h30.

Botha Co-op P O Botha 6857; Tel: (02324) 740. Winemaker: Andre Stofberg. Weekdays 07h30 - 12h30, 13h30 - 17h30 and Saturdays 10h00 - 12h00.

Bottelary Co-op P O Box 16, Koelenhof 7605; Tel: (02231) 92204. Winemaker: Danie Zeeman. Weekdays 08h30 - 12h30, 13h30 - 17h00 and Saturdays 08h30 - 13h00.

Bovlei Co-op P O Box 82, Wellington 7655; Tel: (02211) 31567 or 641283. Winemaker: Martinus Broodryk. Weekdays 08h00 - 12h30, 13h30 - 17h30 and Saturdays 08h30 - 12h30.

Brandvlei Co-op P O Box 595, Worcester, 6850; Tel: (0231) 94215. General Manager: Theuns le Roux; Winemaker: Willie Burger. Weekdays 07h30 - 12h30, 13h30 - 17h30.

Buitenverwachting Klein Constantia Road, Constantia 7800; Tel: (021) 7945190/1. Winemaker: Jean Daneel. Weekdays 09h00-17h00 and Saturdays 11h00-13h00. Cellar tours 11h00 and 15h00 weekdays and 11h00 Saturdays.

Calitzdorp Co-op P O Box 193, Calitzdorp 6660; Tel: (04437) 301 or 328. Winemaker: James O' Kennedy. Weekdays 08h30 - 12h15, 13h15 - 17h00 and Saturdays 08h00 - 12h00.

Chamonix P O Box 28, Franschhoek 7690; Tel: (02212) 2494/2642. Winemakers: Tim and Mike Pickering. Visitors by appointment only. Wine sales and tasting: Franschhoek Vineyards, Le Quartier Français, Die Binnehof.

Citrusdal Co-op P O Box 41, Citrusdal 7340; Tel: (02662) 94/121. Cellar master: Michael de Beer; Manager: Kobus Louw. Weekdays 08h00 - 17h00 and Saturdays 08h30 - 12h30.

Clairvaux Co-op P O Box 179, Robertson 6705; Tel: (02351) 3842. Winemaker: Kobus van der Merwe. Weekdays 08h30 - 12h30, 13h30 - 17h30 and Saturdays 08h30 - 12h00.

Clos Cabrière Estate P O Box 245, Franschhoek 7690; Tel: (02212) 2630. Cellar Master: Pieter Ferreira; Wine grower and Managing Director: Achmin von Arnim. Visitors by appointment only.

Clos Malverné P O Box 187, Stellenbosch; Hovelea Road, off Devon Valley Road, Stellenbosch; Tel: (02231) 3528. Winemaker:

Jeremy Walker; Proprietor: S A Pritchard. Weekdays 08h30 - 17h30 and Saturdays 09h00 - 13h00.

De Doorns Co-op P O Box 129, De Doorns 6875; Tel: (02322) 2100. Winemaker: Pieter Hamman. Weekdays 08h30 - 12h30, 13h30 - 17h00 and Saturdays 08h30 - 12h00.

Delaire Vineyards P O Box 3058, Stellenbosch 7602; Tel: (02231) 91756 or 91335. Winemaker: Mike Dobrovic; Proprietor: Storm Quinan. Visitors by appointment only.

Delheim Wines P O Box 10, Koelenhof 7605; Tel: (02231) 92033. Winemaker: Philip Constandius; Vintner: Spatz Sperling. Wine tasting and sales: weekdays 08h30 - 17h00; Saturdays 08h30 - 12h00. Tours weekdays 10h00 and 15h00, 1 October - 30 April only; tour of production cellar Saturdays all year round 10h30.

De Wet Co-op P O Box 16, De Wet 6853; Tel: (0231) 92710. Winemakers: Jacobus de Wet and Zakkie Bester; Manager: Zakkie Bester. Weekdays 08h30 - 12h00, 13h00 - 17h00.

De Zoete Inval Estate P O Box 591, Suider Paarl 7624; Tel: (02211) 632375. Winemaker: Adrian Frater. Visitors by appointment only.

Die Krans Estate P O Box 28, Calitzdorp 6660; Tel: (04437) 314. Winemakers: Boets and Stroebel Nel. Weekdays 08h30 - 17h00; Saturdays 09h00 - 12h00.

Diemersdal Estate P O Durbanville 7550; Tel: (021) 963361. Winemaker: Tienie Louw. Will be opening to the public in January 1991. Visiting times not yet available.

Die Poort P O Box 45, Albertinia 6795; Tel: (02952) 2030. Winemaker: Jannie Jonker; Proprietor: Jannie Jonker. Weekdays 08h00 - 18h00 and Saturdays 08h00 - 13h00.

Douglas Co-op P O Box 47, Douglas 8730; Tel: (05362) 61. Winemaker: Pou le Roux. Weekdays 08h00 - 13h00, 14h00 - 17h00.

Drakenstein Co-op P O Box 19, Simondium 7670; Tel: (02211) 41051/4. Winemaker: Hein Hesebeck. Weekdays 08h30 - 17h00 and Saturdays 08h30 - 13h00.

Drostdy Co-op P O Box 85, Tulbagh 6820; Tel: (02362) 101/ 525. Winemaker: G Wagener. Weekdays 08h00 - 12h00, 13h30 - 17h00 and Saturdays 08h30 - 12h00.

Domein Doornkraal P O Box 104, De Rust 6650; Tel: (04439) 6715/ 2551. Proprietor: Swepie le Roux; Winemaker: Mr G C le Roux; Weekdays 09h00 - 17h00 and Saturdays 09h00 - 15h00. During holidays open weekdays 08h00 - 18h00.

Du Toitskloof Co-op P O Box 55, Rawsonville 6845; Tel: (0231)

91601. Winemaker: Philip Jordaan. Weekdays 08h30 - 12h30, 13h30 - 17h30 (closes 17h00 on Fridays); Saturdays 08h30 - 12h00.

Eersterivier Valleise Co-op P O Box 2, Vlottenburg 7604; Tel: (02231) 93870/1. Winemaker: Manie Roussouw. Weekdays 08h30 - 12h30, 13h30 - 17h00 and Saturdays 09h00 - 13h00.

Eikendal Vineyards P O Box 2261, Stellenbosch 7600; Tel: (024) 551422. Winemaker: Josef Krammer. Weekdays 09h30 - 17h00 and Saturdays 09h00 - 12h30.

Fairview Estate P O Box 583, Suider Paarl 7625; Tel: (02211) 22367. Winemaker: Charles Back. Weekdays 08h30 - 18h00 and Saturdays 08h30 - 17h00.

Franschhoek Vineyards Co-op P O Box 52, Franschhoek 7690; Tel: (02212) 2086. Winemaker: Deon Truter. Weekdays 08h30 - 13h00, 14h00 - 17h00; Saturdays 09h00 - 13h00. Cellar tours by appointment only.

Gilbeys Limited P O Box 137, Stellenbosch 7600; Tel: (02231) 75036. Cellar master: Martin van der Merwe. Visitors by appointment only.

Goudini Co-op P O Box 132, Rawsonville 6845; Tel: (0231) 91090/91313. Winemaker: Hennie Hugo. Weekdays 08h00 - 12h00, 13h30 - 17h00.

Goudveld Wynkelder P O Box 1091, Welkom 9460; Tel: (0171) 28650. Winemaker: Merkil Alers. Mondays to Saturdays 08h30 - 18h00.

Groot Constantia Estate Private Bag Constantia 7848; Tel: (021) 7945179/7945128. Winemaker: Pieter du Toit; Manager: Danie Appel. Mondays to Sundays 10h00 - 17h00.

Groot Eiland Co-op P O Box 93, Rawsonville 6845; Tel: (0231) 91140. Winemaker: W Loots. Weekdays 08h30 - 12h30, 13h30 - 17h00.

Hamilton Russell Vineyards Oude Hemel en Aarde P O Box 158, Hermanus 7200; Tel: (02831) 23441 or 23440. Winemaker: Peter Finlayson. Visitors by appointment only.

Hartenberg Estate P O Box 69, Koelenhof 7605; Tel: (02231) 92541. Winemaker: Danie Truter. Weekdays 08h30 - 17h00 and Saturdays 09h00 - 14h00. Cellar tours weekdays 10h00 and 15h00, and Saturdays 10h00. Lunch served between 12h00 and 14h00 Monday to Saturday.

Haut Provence P O Box 211, Franschhoek 7690; Tel: (02212) 3195. Proprietor: Peter Younghusband. Wednesdays and Fridays 14h00 - 16h00 and Saturdays 09h30 - 12h00. Open daily from 1 December to 15 April.

Helderberg Co-op P O Box 71, Firgrove 7110; Tel: (024) 422370. Winemaker: Inus Muller. Weekdays 09h00 - 13h00, 14h00 - 17h30 and Saturdays 09h00 - 12h00.

Jacobsdal Co-op P O Box 94, Jacobsdal 8710; Tel: (053212) 132/99. Winemaker: Ian Sieg. Weekdays 08h30 - 13h00, 14h00 - 17h00 and Saturdays 08h30 - 12h00.

Kaapzicht Estate P O Box 5, Sanlamhof 7532; Tel: (021) 9033870. Winemaker: Danie Steytler. Visitors by appointment only.

Kango Co-op P O Box 46, Oudtshoorn 6620; Tel: (04431) 6065/6. Winemaker: C Langenhoven; Manager: Pieter Conradie. Weekdays 08h30 - 13h00, 14h00 - 16h45. Close 16h00 on Fridays.

Kanonkop Estate P O Box 19, Muldersvlei 7606; Tel: (02231) 94656. Winemaker: Beyers Truter. Weekdays 08h30 - 12h30, 13h30 - 16h30 and Saturdays 10h00 - 13h00.

Klawer Co-op P O Box 8, Klawer 8145; Tel: Klawer (02724) 61530. Winemaker: Alkie van der Merwe. Mondays to Thursdays 08h30 - 17h30 and Fridays 08h30 - 17h00.

Klein Constantia Estate P O Box 375, Constantia 7848; Tel: (021) 7945188. Winemaker: Ross Gower. Weekdays 09h00 - 13h00, 14h00 - 17h00 and Saturdays 09h00 - 13h00.

Klein Zalze Estate c/o Gilbeys P O Box 137, Stellenbosch 7600; Tel: (02231) 75036. Winemaker: Marius Lategan. Cellar tours by appointment only.

Koelenhof Co-op P O Box 1, Koelenhof 7605; Tel: (02231) 92020/1. Winemaker: Herman du Preez. Weekdays 08h30 - 13h00, 14h00 - 17h00 and Saturdays 08h30 - 12h30.

Koopmanskloof Estate Koelenhof, 7605; Tel: (02231) 92355. Winemaker: Stevie Smit. Appointments made through Bergkelder.

KWV P O Box 528, Suider Paarl 7624; Tel: (02211) 631001. Winemaker: W F Hacker. Presentations Monday, Wednesday, Friday 09h30 and 14h15 Afrikaans; Monday 11h00 and 15h45 English; Tuesday and Thursday 09h30 and 14h15 English; Tuesday and Thursday 11h00 and 15h45 Afrikaans.

La Bri Franschhoek 7690; Tel: (02212) 2593. Proprietors: Michael and Cheryl Trull. Visitors by appointment only.

Ladismith Co-op P O Box 56, Ladismith 6885; Tel: (02942) 31. Winemaker: Alex Roussouw. Weekdays 08h00 - 12h30, 14h00 - 17h00.

La Motte Estate P O Box 45, La Motte 7691; Tel: (02212) 3119. Winemaker: Jacques Borman. Visitors by appointment only.

Landskroon Estate P O Box 519, Suider Paarl 7624; Tel: (02211)

631039 or 631059. Winemaker: Paul de Villiers Jnr. Weekdays 08h30 - 17h30 and Saturdays 08h30 - 12h30.

Langverwacht Co-op P O Box 87, Bonnievale 6730; Tel: (02346) 2815. Winemaker: Johan Gerber. Weekdays 08h00 - 12h30, 13h30 - 17h00.

La Provence P O Box 188, Franschhoek 7690; Tel: (02212) 2163. Vineyard manager: Freddie Steytler; Winemaker: François Malherbe. Visitors by appointment only.

Lebensraum Estate P O Box 36, Rawsonville 6845; Tel: (0231) 91137. Winemakèr: Philip Deetlefs. Weekdays 14h00 - 18h00.

Lemberg Estate P O Box 108, Tulbagh 6820; Tel: (02362) 2311. Winemaker: Janey Muller. Visitors by appointment only.

Les Chênes P O Box 221, Franschhoek 7690; Tel: (02212) 2498. Proprietor: Sarel van Vuuren; Winemaker: Dion Truter. Visitors by appointment only. Wine tasting at the Franschhoek Wine Centre.

Lievland P O Box 66, Klapmuts 7625; Tel: (02211) 5226. Winemaker: Abraham Beukes. Weekdays 09h00 - 17h00, Saturdays 09h00 - 13h00.

Loopspruit Winery P O Box 1531, Bronkhorstspruit 1020; Tel: (01212) 24303. Winemaker: S F Conradie. Mondays to Fridays 08h00 - 17h00 and Saturdays 09h00 - 13h00.

L'Ormarins Estate Private Bag Suider Paarl 7624; Tel: (02211) 41024. Winemakers: Anthonij Rupert and Nico Vermeulen. Weekdays 08h30 - 17h00; Saturdays 08h30 - 12h30 for visitors, but not for sales.

Louwshoek-Voorsorg Co-op P O Box 174, Rawsonville, 6845; Tel: (0231) 91110. Winemaker: Jaco Potgieter. Weekdays 08h00 - 12h30, 13h30 - 17h00.

Lutzville Co-op P O Box 50, Lutzville 8165; Tel: (02725) 71516. Winemaker: Johan Theron. Weekdays 08h00 - 13h00, 14h00 - 17h00 and Saturdays 08h00 - 12h00.

Mamreweg Co-op P O Box 114, Darling 7345; Tel: (02241) 2276/7. Winemaker: François Weich. Mondays to Thursdays 08h30 - 17h30; closes at 16h00 on Fridays. Saturdays 09h00 - 12h00.

McGregor Co-op Private Bag X619, Robertson 6705; Tel: (02353) 741. Winemaker: Carel van der Merwe. Weekdays 08h00 - 12h00, 13h00 - 17h00.

Meerlust Estate P O Box 15, Faure 7131; Tel: (024) 43587. Winemakers: Giorgio Dalla Cia and Hannes Myburgh. Visitors by appointment only.

Merwespont Co-op P O Box 68, Bonnievale 6730; Tel: (02346)

2800. Winemaker: Dirk Cornelissen. Weekdays 07h30 - 12h30, 13h30 - 17h00.

Merwida Co-op P O Box 4, Rawsonville 6845; Tel: (0231) 91301. Winemaker: Jacobus Wolhuter. Weekdays 07h30 - 12h00; 13h30 - 17h30.

Mon Don Estate P O Box 360, Robertson 6705; Tel: (02351) 4183/2720. Winemaker: Pierre Marais. Weekdays 09h00 - 12h00, 14h00 - 16h00.

Montagu Muskadel Boere Co-op P O Box 29, Montagu 6720; Tel: (0234) 41125. Winemaker: Sonnie Malan. Weekdays 08h30 - 12h30, 13h30 - 17h00.

Montpellier Estate P O Box 24, Tulbagh 6820; Tel: (02362) 3904. Winemaker: Jan Theron. Weekdays 09h00 - 12h00,14h00 - 16h30 and Saturdays 10h00 - 12h00.

Mooiuitsig Wynkelders P O Box 15, Bonnievale 6730; Tel: (02346) 2143. Winemakers: Chris Versveld and Francois Claasen; Managing Director: Boet Jonker. Weekdays 08h00 - 17h30.

Morgenhof P O Box 365, Stellenbosch 7600; Tel: (02231) 95510. Winemaker: Pietie Theron. Weekdays 09h00 - 16h30 and Saturdays 09h00 - 12h30. Cellar tours by appointment.

Moutonne-Excelsior P O Box 290, Franschhoek 7690; Tel: (02212) 3019/2071. Winetastings at Die Binnehof daily except Mondays.

Muratie Estate P O Box 9, Koelenhof 7605; Tel: (02231) 92330/92396. Winemaker: Christo Hedder. Weekdays 08h00 - 12h00,13h00 - 17h00; closes 16h00 on Fridays. Saturdays 08h00 - 12h00.

Mons Ruber Estate Private Bag X629, Oudtshoorn 6620; Tel: (04439) 6812. Winemaker: Raadie Meyer. Weekdays 08h30 - 17h00 and Saturdays 08h30 - 13h00.

Nederburg Wines P O Box 46, Huguenot, Paarl 7645; Tel: (02211) 623104. Winemaker: Newald Marais. For daily tours, phone to book. Weekdays 08h30 - 13h00, 14h00 - 16h30.

Neethlingshof Estate P O Box 104, Stellenbosch 7600; Tel: (02231) 76832. Winemaker: Johannes Louwrens; Director: Günter Brözel. Weekdays 08h30 - 17h00 and Saturdays 08h30 - 12h00. Cellar Tours 11h30 and 15h30. No cellar tours on Saturdays or public holidays.

Nordale Co-op P O Box 105, Bonnievale 6730; Tel: (02346) 2050. Winemaker: L E Schoch. Weekdays 08h00 - 12h30, 13h30 - 17h00.

Nuy Co-op P O Nuy 6700; Tel: (0231) 70272. Winemaker: Wilhelm Linde. Weekdays 08h30 - 16h30, Saturdays 08h30 - 12h30.

Opstal Estate P O Box 27, Rawsonville 6845; Tel: (0231) 91066. Winemaker: Stanley Louw. Weekdays 09h00 - 11h00, 15h00 - 17h00.
Oranjerivier Wynkelders P O Box 544, Upington 8800; Tel: (0541) 25651. General Manager: Noel Mouton. Weekdays 08h00 - 12h45, 14h00 - 17h00 and Saturdays 08h30 - 13h00.
Oude Nektar Estate P O Box 389, Stellenbosch 7600; Tel: (02231) 70690. Winemaker: Peter Peck. Weekdays 09h30 - 17h00 and Saturdays 09h30 - 12h30. (Closed from April to August.)
Overgaauw Estate P O Box 3, Vlottenburg 7604; Tel: (02231) 93815. Winemaker: Braam van Velden. Weekdays 09h00 - 12h30, 14h00 - 17h00 and Saturdays 10h00 - 12h00.
Overhex Co-op P O Box 139, Worcester 6850; Tel: (0231) 71057. Winemaker: Doug Lawrie. Weekdays 07h30 - 12h30, 14h00 - 17h30.
Perdeberg Co-op P O Box 214, Paarl 7621; Tel: (02211) 638112. Winemaker: Joseph Huskisson. Weekdays 08h00 - 12h30, 14h00 - 17h00.
Porterville Co-op P O Box 52, Porterville 6810; Tel: (02623) 2170. Winemaker: Klaas de Jongh. Weekdays 08h30 - 13h00, 14h00 - 17h00 and Saturdays 08h30 - 12h00.
Rhebokskloof P O Box 2125, Windmeul 7630; Tel (02211) 638386/638504. Winemaker: Ernst Grouws. Weekdays 08h00 - 17h00. Tours of the property by appointment.
Riebeek Wine Farmers' Co-op P O Box 13, Riebeek-Kasteel 6801; Tel: (02244) 213/281. Winemaker: Sias du Toit. Weekdays 07h30 - 12h30, 13h30 - 17h30, Saturdays 08h30 - 12h00.
Rietrivier Co-op P O Box 144, Montagu 6720; Tel: (0234) 41705. Winemaker: Piet Frick. Weekdays 08h00 - 13h00, 14h00 - 17h00 and Saturdays 08h00 - 11h00.
Robertson Co-op P O Box 37, Robertson 6705; Tel: (02351) 3059. Winemaker: Bowen Botha. Mondays to Thursdays 08h30 - 12h30, 13h30 - 17h00. Closes at 16h30 on Fridays.
Romansrivier Co-op P O Box 108, Wolseley 6830; Tel: (023232) 242 or 352. Winemakers: Olla Olivier and Jako Smit. Weekdays 08h30 - 12h00, 13h30 - 17h00.
Roodezandt Co-op P O Box 164, Robertson 6705; Tel: (02351) 2912 or 3020. Winemaker: Christie Steytler; Manager: Robbie Roberts. Weekdays 08h30 - 13h00, 14h00 - 17h30 and Saturdays 08h30 - 12h30.
Rooiberg Co-op P O Box 358, Robertson 6705; Tel: (02351) 2322/2312. Winemaker: Tommy Loftus; Cellar master: Dassie

Smith. Weekdays 08h00 - 17h30, Saturdays 08h00 - 13h00.

Rustenberg Wines (*see* **Schoongezicht**)

Rust-en-Vrede Estate P O Box 473, Stellenbosch 7600; Tel: (02231) 93881/93757. Winemaker: Kevin Arnold. Weekdays 08h30 - 12h30, 13h30 - 16h30 and Saturdays 09h00 - 12h00.

Saxenheim P O Box 171, Kuilsrivier 7580; Tel: (021) 9036113. Winemaker: Andre van Rensburg. Weekdays 08h00 - 17h00 and Saturdays 09h00 - 13h00.

Schoongezicht Estate P O Box 33, Stellenbosch 7600; Tel: (02231) 73153. Winemaker: Etienne le Riche. Weekdays 08h30 - 17h00.

Simonsig Estate P O Box 6, Koelenhof 7605; Tel: (02231) 92443/92044. Winemaker: Johan Malan. Weekdays 08h30 - 13h00, 14h00 - 17h00 (mid-season open during lunch times); Saturdays 08h30 - 12h30. Cellar tours 10h00 and 15h00.

Simonsvlei Co-op P O Box 584, Suider Paarl 7624; Tel: (02211) 633040. Winemaker: Kobus Roussouw. Weekdays 08h30 - 17h00 and Saturdays 08h30 - 13h00.

Slanghoek Co-op P O Box 75, Rawsonville 6845; Tel: (0231) 91130. Winemaker: Bill Pretorius. Weekdays 07h30 - 12h30, 13h30 - 17h30. Closes 16h30 on Fridays. Saturdays 09h00 - 12h00.

Soetwynboere Co-op P O Box 127, Montagu 6720; Tel: (0234) 41340. Winemaker: Kenneth Knipe. Weekdays 08h00 - 12h30, 13h30 - 17h00 and Saturdays 08h00 - 11h00.

Spier Estate P O Box 28, Vlottenburg 7604; Tel: (02231) 93808/9. Winemaker: Jan Smit; Vintner: Chris Joubert. Weekdays 08h30 - 17h00 and Saturdays 08h30 - 13h00.

Spruitdrift Co-op P O Box 129, Vredendal 8160; Tel: (0271) 33086/7. Winemaker: Johan Roussouw. Weekdays 08h30 - 12h30, 14h00 - 17h30 and Saturdays 08h30 - 11h00.

Stellenbosch Farmers' Winery (SFW) P O Box 46, Stellenbosch 7600; Tel: (02231) 73400. Production manager: Duimpie Bayly. No cellar sales. For daily tours, phone to book.

Swartland Co-op P O Box 95, Malmesbury 7300; Tel: (0224) 21434/21134. Winemakers: Johan de Villiers and Christo Koch. Production manager: Albie van Vuuren. Weekdays 08h00 - 13h00, 14h00 - 17h00 and Saturdays 09h00 - 12h00.

Stellenzicht P O Box 104, Stellenbosch 7600; Tel: (02231) 901103. Winemaker: Marinus Bredell. Not open to the public, but visits can be arranged by appointment.

Thelema P O Box 2234, Dennesig 7601; Tel: (02231) 91924.

Winemaker: Gyles Webb. Weekdays 09h00 - 12h00, 14h00 - 17h00. Saturdays by appointment only.

Theuniskraal Estate Tulbagh 6820; Tel: (02362) 2740. Winemaker: Kobus Jordaan. Not open to the public, but visits can be arranged by appointment.

Twee Jongegezellen P O Box 16, Tulbagh 6820; Tel: (02362) 2603/4. Winemaker: Nicky Krone. Visitors by special appointment.

Uiterwyk Estate P O Box 15, Vlottenburg 7604; Tel: (02331) 93711. Winemaker: Chris de Waal. Weekdays 09h00 - 12h00, 14h00 - 16h30. Saturdays 10h00 - 12h00 (December to February).

Vaalharts Co-op P O Box 4, Hartswater 8570; Tel: (05332) 425111/42569. Winemaker: Roelof Maree. Weekdays 08h00 - 17h00 and Saturdays 08h00 - 12h00.

Van Loveren P O Box 19, Klaasvoogds 6707; Tel: (0234) 51505. Winemaker: Wynand Retief. Weekdays 08h30 - 13h00, 14h00 - 17h00 and Saturdays 09h30 - 13h00.

Vergenoegd Estate P O Box 1, Faure 7131; Tel: (024) 43248. Winemakers: Jac and John Faure. Wednesdays 14h00 - 17h00.

Villiera Estate P O Box 66, Koelenhof 7605; Tel: (02231) 92002/3. Cellar master: Jeff Grier. Weekdays 08h30 - 17h00 and Saturdays 08h30 -12h30.

Villiersdorp Co-op P O Box 14, Villiersdorp 7170; Tel: (0225) 31120. Winemaker: J P Steenekamp. Weekdays 08h00 - 13h00, 14h00 - 17h00 and Saturdays 08h00 - 11h00.

Vlottenburg Co-op P O Box 40, Vlottenburg 7604; Tel: (02231) 93828/9. Winemaker: Kowie du Toit. Weekdays 08h00 - 17h00 and Saturdays 09h00 - 12h30.

Vredendal Co-op P O Box 75, Vredendal 8160; Tel: (0271) 31080. Winemaker: Giel Swiegers. Weekdays 08h00 - 12h30, 14h00 - 17h30 and Saturdays 08h00 - 12h00.

Vredenheim Estate Wines (Made on the farm Vredenburg) P O Box 369, Stellenbosch 7600; Tel: (02231) 93673/93878. Proprietor: C J Bezuidenhout. Weekdays 09h00 - 16h00. Saturdays 09h00 - 12h00 (December and January).

Waboomsrivier Co-op P O Box 24, Bre-rivier 6858; Tel: (02324) 730. Winemakers: Chris van der Merwe and Jaco Bruwer. Weekdays 08h30 - 17h00 and Saturdays 08h30 - 10h00.

Wamakers Vallei Co-op P O Box 509, Wellington 7657; Tel: (02211) 31582. Winemaker: Chris Roux. Weekdays 08h00 - 12h30, 14h00 - 17h00.

Warwick Farm P O Box 2, Muldersvlei 7606; Tel: (02231) 94410. Winemaker: Norma Ratcliffe. Visitors by appointment only.

Welgemeend Estate P O Box 69, Klapmuts 7625; Tel: (02211) 5210. Winemaker: Billy Hofmeyr. Saturdays 09h00 - 12h30.

Wellington Wynboere Co-op P O Box 520, Wellington 7657; Tel: (02211) 31163. Winemaker: Gert Boerssen. Weekdays 08h00 - 12h30, 14h00 - 17h30; closes at 17h00 on Fridays.

Welmoed Co-op P O Box 23, Lyndoch 7603; Tel: (02231) 93800/1. Winemaker: Nicky Versveld. Weekdays and Saturdays 08h30 - 17h00.

Weltevrede Estate P O Box 6, Bonnievale 6730; Tel: (02346) 2141/2146. Winemaker: Gerhardt van Deventer. Weekdays 08h30 - 13h00, 14h00 - 17h00; Saturdays 09h30 - 11h30. Cellar tours by appointment.

Windmeul Co-op P O Box 2031, Windmeul 7630; Tel: (02211) 638043/638100. Winemaker: Hein Koegelenberg; Manager: Bernhard Luttich. Weekdays 08h00 - 12h30, 13h30 - 17h00.

Zandvliet Estate P O Box 36, Ashton 6715; Tel: (0234) 51146/51823. Winemaker: Paul de Wet Jnr. Not open to the public. Cellar tours by appointment only.

Zevenwacht P O Box 387, Kuilsrivier 7580; Tel: (021) 9035123. Winemaker: Eric Saayman. Weekdays 08h30 - 12h30, 13h30 - 17h00; Saturdays 09h00 - 12h30.

GLOSSARY

ACIDITY: Grapes contain acids which remain in the juice after pressing. A good wine has a fine balance between fruit sugar and acid. High acidity results in sharp wines, while a too low acidity results in soft, sometimes uninteresting wine.

ACETOBACTER: A mould which occurs naturally on grape skins and produces acetic acid, or vinegar. Acetobacters are killed off early in the winemaking process, by adding sulphur dioxide to the must.

ALCOHOL: Alcohol is the result of fermentation and is formed by the action of yeast on sugar. It gives wine its body and character and acts as a preservative. There are several kinds of alcohol, but the one found in wine and spirits is ethyl alcohol.

AROMA: A term used to describe the fragrance the wine gets from the fruit. Not to be confused with 'bouquet,' which is the fragrance obtained from fermentation and maturation.

ASTRINGENCY: The quality of a wine which makes the inside of the mouth pucker. An astringent character comes from the tannins in the grape skins and stalks. A very astringent wine will probably last a long time in the bottle, becoming smoother and softer with age.

BALTHAZAR: A huge wine bottle, containing the equivalent of 16 normal bottles of wine.

BENTONITE: A type of clay used in the clarification, or fining, of wines. It has no effect on the flavour of the wine.

BLANC DE BLANC: A white wine made from white grape varieties.

BLANC DE NOIR: A white wine made from red grape varieties. The juice is removed from the skins before it has had time to pick up any of the red colouring. In fact, most winemakers allow the juice to pick up a small amount of colouring to produce the characteristic 'onion-skin' colour associated with blancs de noir.

BLANC FUMÉ: A name sometimes given to wine made from Sauvignon Blanc grapes. In South Africa blanc fumé is usually matured in wood, but not necessarily always so. There are some unwooded blanc fumés on the market.

BLENDING: The art of mixing wines of different cultivars - or from different vintages or areas - to achieve a particular style of wine.

BOUQUET: The fragrance in wine derived from fermentation, maturation and ageing. Not the same as 'Aroma'.

BRUT: A French term for 'dry', usually applied to sparkling wine with a sugar content of less than 1,5 percent.

CAPSULE: The plastic or lead cap placed over the cork in a bottle of wine.

CARBONIC MACERATION: A winemaking method involving the fermentation of whole bunches of grapes in an atmosphere of carbon dioxide. Used in the production of 'Beaujolais Nouveau' style wines, designed to be drunk very fresh and young.

CHARMAT PROCESS: A method of producing sparkling wine in the tank by trapping the carbon dioxide produced in the fermentation process. The resulting wine is then bottled under pressure.

CLARITY: Clean and bright, not cloudy or dull.

COOPERAGE: The craft of making and repairing wooden barrels. At one stage the craft almost died out, as alternate methods of storing wine were developed. Recently, however, wood maturation has become very fashionable and coopers are once again in demand.

CORKED WINE: A microbial infection of a cork can give a disagreeable smell and flavour to the wine, known as 'corkiness'.

CULTIVAR: A term used in South Africa for a grape variety or varietal, used in viticulture. Chenin Blanc and Cabernet Sauvignon, for example, are cultivars.

CUVÉE: Literally, the contents of a cask. Now generally used to denote the base wine from which sparkling wine will be made.

DECANTING: The process of carefully pouring wine from one container (usually the bottle) into another (usually a decanter) in order to separate the wine from any sediment which may have formed in the bottle, and also to aerate the wine.

DINKY: A small wine bottle containing 250ml of wine, often sold on airlines (you know you're in trouble when you step shakily off the plane with your pockets bulging). Dinkies are fitted with metal screw-caps, rather than corks.

EXTRACT: The soluble solids that are non-volatile and non-sugars. Wines with a high extract have a very intense, concentrated flavour.

FAREWELL: A term used to describe the flavour as well as the length of time the flavour remains in the mouth after the wine has been swallowed. Sometimes referred to as the 'aftertaste'.

FILTERING: A method of removing impurities or small particles from wine by pumping it through a filter membrane.

FINING: A method of clarifying wine by adding a substance like egg white or bentonite, which sinks slowly to the bottom of the tank, taking suspended particles with it.

FINO: A term used to describe a very dry, light style of sherry.

FLOR: A strain of yeast used in the making of sherry. Unlike most yeasts, flor yeast floats to the top of the fermenting wine.

FORTIFIED WINES: Wines made by the addition of brandy spirit to fermenting wine. Fortified wines include sherries, port and dessert wines. Popular locally are the sweet Muscadels and jerepigos from our warmer wine producing regions.

FRUITY: A wine is said to be fruity when it gives off a distinctive fruity aroma - not necessarily grapes. Steen wines, for example, often smell of guavas, while others have the aroma of blackberries or even pineapples.

FULL-BODIED: A wine high in flavour components. Usually a very 'mouth-filling' wine.

GOOD WINE: A term used in South Africa to denote wine made for drinking, as opposed to 'rebate wine' which is made for distilling into brandy.

HEAVY: A term used to describe a wine with a high alcohol content and strong flavours. Such a wine usually needs time to mellow.

HORIZONTAL TASTING: A tasting at which wines from the same vintage, but from different producers or areas, are compared. Not to be confused with horizontal tasters, who are tasters who have sampled a great many wines without spitting them out!

JEROBOAM: A large bottle, which contains the equivalent of four regular bottles of wine.

LEES: The sediment - consisting mainly of dead yeast cells - which remains after fermentation has taken place.

LEGS: The tear-drop shaped runnels of wine which adhere to the sides of the tasting glass after the wine has been swirled.

MAGNUM: A wine bottle which holds the equivalent of two normal bottles - 1,5 litres.

MALOLACTIC FERMENTATION: Also known as secondary fermentation. This sometimes occurs after the wine has been fermented, and is the process by which malic acid is converted to the softer lactic acid. It is often induced by the winemaker to obtain a smoother, less acidic wine.

MATURATION: The process whereby wines are left in wooden casks or bottles to age, improve and mellow. The period of maturation depends on the type of wine. Some heavy reds need a decade or more before they reach their peak of smoothness.

MELLOW: Wine that has softened by ageing. Also, a mood induced by drinking such wine.

MÉTHODE CHAMPENOISE: A complicated and time-consuming method traditionally used in the Champagne area of France to produce the famous sparkling Champagne. Sugar is added to the bottled wine, causing a second fermentation, and the carbon dioxide thus produced is trapped in the bottles. After allowing the dead yeast to settle on the cork, it is removed by freezing the bottle neck and letting the pressure blow out the frozen plug of yeast. The bottle is then topped up and re-sealed and is then ready for market.

METHUSELAH: A large wine bottle containing the equivalent of eight normal sized bottles.

MUST: The liquid obtained by crushing grapes. Must does not contain skins or pips. Probably best known in South Africa by its Afrikaans name, 'mos', and used in the preparation of 'moskonfyt' and 'mosbolletjies' at harvest time.

NATURAL WINE: Quite simply, an unfortified wine to which nothing has been added.

NEBUCHADNEZZAR: The largest size of wine bottle made. It contains the equivalent of 20 normal sized bottles of wine.

NOBLE: A term meaning well-bred or classy. Some grape varieties are referred to as 'noble varieties', but there is much argument about which are noble and which are not. It's safer to stay out of this one.

NOSE: A term applied to the bouquet and aroma of the wine. A wine with a 'good nose' is one that is pleasant to smell. Testing the aroma and bouquet is known as 'nosing' the wine.

OENOLOGY: The science of winemaking - in the cellar - as opposed to viticulture, which is the science of vineyard production.

OLD BROWN: A dark coloured, very sweet style of sherry.

OLOROSO: A term used to describe a sweetish style of sherry.

ORGANOLEPTIC: A scientific word for the evaluation of wine by tasting, examining and smelling it. If you say you're giving the wine an 'organoleptic assessment', it's a fancy way of saying you're tasting it.

OXIDISED: A fault in wine owing to excessive exposure to air, and which can be detected on both nose and palate.

PALATE: Your palate is actually the roof of your mouth, but somebody who has a fine sense of taste, as far as wine is concerned, is said to have a 'good palate'.

PERLÉ: Slightly effervescent wine, as opposed to sparkling wine, which effervesces vigorously.

PETILLANT: A term used to describe wine which has a very slight sparkle to it - probably more of a twinkle than a sparkle. If it had slightly more bubbles, it would be a perlé wine.

pH: The strength of acidity or alkalinity in a wine. Wines with a pH of more than 7 are alkaline, while those with a pH of less than 7 are acid. The lower the figure, the stronger the acid. A low pH helps to prevent bacterial spoilage and gives the wine a good colour.

PIPE: An oak cask that tapers strongly towards the ends, used for storing port.

PORT: A fortified wine, originally produced in the Duoro Valley of Portugal and shipped from Oporto. Most wine producing countries make red and white port. In South Africa very little white port is consumed, except in Natal, where it is surprisingly quite popular.

PREMIER GRAND CRU: A rather meaningless term, used in South Africa simply to describe a very dry white wine.

PUNT: The indentation in the bottom of some bottles. Originally introduced to strengthen the bottle.

RACKING: A method of clarifying wine by drawing it off from the tank, leaving the sediment, or lees, behind.

REMUAGE: The gentle shaking and twisting of sparkling wine bottles in their racks to move the sediment gradually down to rest on the temporary closure.

RESIDUAL SUGAR: If the winemaking process is stopped before all the sugar has been converted to alcohol, the sugar remaining in the wine is known as residual sugar.

RHEBOAM: A large bottle which contains the equivalent of six normal bottles of wine.

ROSÉ: Rosé wines are made by allowing the red grapes to ferment for just a few hours on the skins. Once the juice is an attractive pink colour, it is separated from the skins.

SALMANAZAR: A large wine bottle containing the equivalent of 12 bottles of wine.

SEMI-SWEET: A term used in South Africa to describe a wine that has more than four grams of residual sugar, but not more than 30 grams per litre.

SOLERA CELLAR: A system of wooden casks arranged in tiers, for the making of sherry. Wine is drawn from the bottom casks, which are then topped up from the row above them, and those in turn topped up from those above. This is why sherry is never given a vintage. The whole sherry-making cycle takes about seven years.

SOUR: Sour wine is wine that has begun to turn to vinegar. Not to be confused with dry wine or acidic wine.

SPARKLING WINE: Wine that has an effervescence, due to the presence of carbon dioxide. This can be from the fermentation process, or may be added to the wine after fermentation.

STABILISATION: Before cold stabilisation was introduced, wines often produced a sediment of tartrate crystals, which caused cloudiness, and meant the wine had to be decanted before drinking. Modern wines are usually stabilised by chilling the tank to about four degrees celsius, which causes the tartrate crystals to form and sink to the bottom of the tank. The wine is then bottled without fear of further crystals forming in the bottle.

STEEN: The old South African name for Chenin Blanc, the most widely planted wine grape cultivar in this country. Not to be confused with 'Stein', a semi-sweet wine originally made in Germany. You can, of course, make a stein from Steen grapes.

SULPHUR DIOXIDE: A gas used to sterilise the wine and kill natural yeasts. In South Africa very low levels of sulphur dioxide are used in the making of wine. Some people claim that it is the sulphur dioxide that gives them hangovers. Actually, it is too much alcohol that causes hangovers.

TANNIC: Tannic wines contain a good deal of tannin, the astringent substance which comes from the skins and stalks of the grapes. Red wines contain more tannin than whites, because of their long contact with the skins. Tannin acts as a preservative.

TART: A natural and often pleasantly fresh fruity-acid taste in wine.

THIN: Lacking in alcohol, watery or feeble wine.

TAWNY: A term used to describe the colour of an old wine that has changed from purplish red to brownish due to maturation. Also used to describe a type of port.

VARIETAL: Another word for 'cultivar' or grape variety. A wine can also be said to have a 'varietal character' when it is typical of wines made from that particular cultivar.

VERTICAL TASTING: A wine tasting at which wines of the same cultivar or brand, but from different vintages, are compared.

VERMOUTH: A fortified wine flavoured with aromatic herbs. Sometimes mixed with gin to make a martini.

VINICULTURE: A general term used to denote the whole of the winemaking process, from the planting of the vines to the making of the wine.

VIN ORDINAIRE: An inexpensive, everyday wine, sometimes sold in a carafe or by the glass. Often rudely known as 'plonk'.

VINTAGE: The year in which a wine was made. A 'vintage year' is also used to describe a particularly good year, which produced excellent wines.

In South Africa, a 'vintage wine' is one which contains only the juice of grapes picked in a single harvesting season. If juice from another season is included in the blend, the wine is known as a 'non-vintage' wine.

VOLATILE ACID: The acid of vinegar - acetic acid. It develops in wine after fermentation and can be quite pleasant in very small quantities, but larger amounts of VA result in an unpleasant, vinegary character.

WOOD MATURATION: The ageing of wine for a time in wooden casks or vats. This gives the wine a rich, oak flavour, sometimes described as a 'vanilla' flavour. Wood maturation is usually given to good red wines, but an increasing number of white wines - notably Chardonnays and Sauvignon Blancs - are now being matured for a while in wood to add complexity.

ZINFANDEL: A wine grape variety not very widely grown in South Africa, but well known in California. Zinfandel is also an extremely useful word for authors who wish to compile an 'A to Z of wine terms' in books about wine.

INDEX

Enjoy Wine

A South African Guide to Unpretentious Winedrinking

David Biggs says he fell into the wine world quite by accident. As an entertainment journalist, he was invited to attend a wine course in Stellenbosch in 1979, and was immediately hooked for life.

As a wine writer and columnist for *The Argus*, he has delighted Capetonians with his quick wit and sharp observations daily.

The light and informal tone of his column has successfully spilled over into *Enjoy Wine*. The style is witty and chatty, yet concise and comprehensive. Aimed at a multitude of amateur wine lovers, *Enjoy Wine* presents aspects of wine drinking from as basic as selecting wine and the correct glasses to use, to a fascinating peek at the year of an average wine farmer.

With the help of respected wine fundi, Dave Hughes, David Biggs has produced a wealth of information for both the seasoned and the uninitiated wine drinker. Interesting facts about the history of the industry and techniques of wine tasting and assessment are balanced by spontaneous remarks, personal opinions and useful hints on drinking wine, serving wine and, most importantly, enjoying wine.

The content includes a history of wine-making, the practicalities of collecting and drinking wine, and the process which results in finely bottled table wines - reds, whites and fortified wines. Recommended reading for anyone who has ever sipped a rare Cabernet or guzzled down a cheap plonk.

ISBN 0-86978-503-6

9 780869 785034